The Martini

BARNABY CONRAD III

THE
Martini

An Illustrated History of an
American Classic

CHRONICLE BOOKS

SAN FRANCISCO

FOR MARTIN MULLER,
A GREAT FRIEND

Library of Congress Cataloging-in-Publication Data Available.
ISBN: 0-8118-0717-7

Printed in Hong Kong.
Book and cover design: Tom Morgan, Blue Design.

Cover photograph by John William Lund.

Distributed in Canada by Raincoast Books,
8680 Cambie Street, Vancouver, B.C., V6P 6M9

10 9 8 7 6 5 4 3 2

Chronicle Books
275 Fifth St.
San Francisco, CA 94103

Grateful acknowledgment is made for the following:

"Martini Scandal," by Russell Baker. Copyright © 1965 by the New York Times Company. Reprinted by permission.

"The Three Martini Debate," by Christopher Buckley. Copyright © 1992 Christopher Buckley. Originally published in *The New Yorker.*

Reprinted with permission of Scribner, an imprint of Simon & Schuster, from *The Sun Also Rises*, by Ernest Hemingway. Copyright © 1926 by Charles Scribner's Sons. Copyright © renewed 1954 by Ernest Hemingway.

Reprinted with permission of Scribner, an imprint of Simon & Schuster, from *Across the River and Into the Trees*, by Ernest Hemingway. Copyright © 1950 by Ernest Hemingway. Copyright renewed © 1978 by Mary Hemingway.

"A Drink with Something in It," copyright © 1938 by Ogden Nash, renewed. Reprinted by permission of Little, Brown and Company and Curtis Brown Ltd.

"To the Gibson and Beyond," by M. F. K. Fisher in the *Atlantic Monthly*. Copyright © M.F.K Fisher. Reprinted with permission.

"For The Wayward and Beguiled," by Bernard DeVoto. Copyright © 1949 by *Harper's* magazine. All rights reserved. Reproduced from the December 1949 issue by special permission.

"Casino Royale," by Ian Fleming. Copyright © Glidrose Publications Ltd 1953.

My Last Sigh, by Luis Buñuel. Copyright © 1983 by Luis Buñuel. Translation copyright by Alfred A. Knopf. Reprinted with permission by Alfred A. Knopf.

Picture Credits:

Associated Press, Ric Feld, page: 76 right. *Author's collection,* pages: 8, 20, 21, 24, 25, 29, 37, 38 bottom, 47, 48 left, 48 right, 61, 64, 78, 81, 88, 89, 91, 105, 108, 122, 125 top, 125 bottom, 126. *The Bettmann Archives, New York,* pages: 10, 16 right, 18, 21 top, 22, 28, 31 bottom, 33, 37, 46 bottom, 60 top, 107, 123 right. *UPI/Bettmann,* pages: 31 top, 34, 35 bottom, 36, 38 top, 41, 50 bottom, 67, 68 bottom, 69, 72, 74 bottom, 76 left, 79, 85 top, 85 bottom, 102, 104, 109. *Bettmann/Hulton,* pages: 11 bottom, 35 top. *Springer/Bettmann Film Archive,* pages: 40, 54, 55, 60 bottom, 63, 65. *Culver Pictures, New York,* pages: 5, 9, 11 top, 16 left, 20 bottom, 42, 43, 56 top, 56 bottom, 100, 103, 123 left. *Metro-Goldwyn-Mayer,* page: 53. *Richard Fishman Collection;* page: 117. *Print Collection, Miriam and Ira D. Wallach Division of Art, Prints, and Photographs, NY Public Library, Astor, Lenox and Tilden Foundations,* page: 124. *Random House ©Joyce Ravid, (Buckley, Thank You For Smoking),* page: 75. *Franklin Roosevelt Library, Hyde Park, NY,* pages: 66, 68 top. *Bert Stern Productions,* page: 74 top. *Shooting Star, Los Angeles,* pages: 6, 45, 50 top, 51 bottom, 52 bottom, 59, 62. *Time/Life,* pages: 14–15.

Page 2: Guy Diehl, Still Life with Martini and Ian Fleming, *1994, acrylic on canvas, 14 x 16 inches. (Modernism Gallery, San Francisco)*

Opposite: The Stork Club's famed bartender, Johnny Brooks, in the 1940s.

Page 6: Cary Grant and Deborah Kerr in An Affair to Remember, *1957.*

Table of Contents

A Dry
Introduction

With a Twist

IT WAS 1935 IN HOLLYWOOD, AND MGM WAS MAKING *China Seas*, starring Clark Gable and Jean Harlow. Robert Benchley, a featured player, was required to spend most of the day floating in the studio's water tank. When he was finally allowed to climb ashore he reputedly announced, "I must get out of these wet clothes and into a dry Martini."

Robert Benchley

Never mind that publisher Bennett Cerf later claimed that the event happened at Cerf's house and not on a movie set, or that Alexander Woollcott, Charles Butterworth, Charles Brackett, and Mae West have also been given credit for the line both on and off screen. The magic phrase sums up the Dry Martini's enduring allure: A few ounces of gin and vermouth—properly mixed, of course— could miraculously banish the shabby worries, the dreadful *ambitions*, of the day. As the barman in his crisp white jacket inquired, "With an olive or twist, sir?" you would be conveyed to a higher plane, where witty conversation, romance, and good fortune flourished.

Dixie Bell Gin advertisement, 1942.

9

The word *Martini* is a nostalgic passport to another era—when automobiles had curves like Mae West, when women were either ladies or dames, when men wore hats, when a deal was done on a handshake, when boxing and polo were regular pastimes, when we lived for movies instead of MTV, and when jazz was going from hot to cool. It was a time when a relationship was called either a romance or an affair, when love over a pitcher of Martinis was bigger than both of us, sweetheart, and it wouldn't matter if the Russians dropped the bomb as long as the gin was wet and the vermouth was dry. That was Martini Culture.

Although a Martini prototype purportedly appeared as early as 1862, the drink came of age in the twentieth century, and by the First World War it was *the* American cocktail. Bernard DeVoto pronounced the Martini nothing less than the "supreme American gift to world culture," and H.L. Mencken declared it "the only American invention as perfect as a sonnet." *New Yorker* writer E.B. White proudly admitted that he drank Martinis "the

E.B. White called Martinis "the elixir of quietude."

way other people take aspirin," imbibing them at lunch and dinner until he was well into his eighties. "Martinis . . . have a muting effect on the constant ringing in my ears, and as five o'clock approaches, my thoughts turn toward the elixir of quietude. Gin stops the bell from tolling."

Hemingway's war-weary heroes drank Martinis whenever they needed a taste of "civilization," and Ian Fleming's James Bond drank them shaken not stirred. Personalities as different as financier John D. Rockefeller, actor William Holden, and Secretary of State Dean Acheson swore by the Martini's superiority over other cocktails. History was made when Franklin Roosevelt plied Stalin with a Martini at the 1943 Teheran Conference, and later Nikita Khrushchev declared the Martini "America's lethal weapon."

I like to have a Martini
Two at the very most—
After three I'm under the table,
After four I'm under my host.
— Dorothy Parker

"A Drink with Something in It"

There is something about a Martini,
A tingle remarkably pleasant;
A yellow, a mellow Martini;
I wish I had one at present.
There is something about a Martini,
Ere the dining and dancing begin,
And to tell you the truth,
It is not the vermouth—
I think that perhaps it's the gin.
—Ogden Nash (1935)

Hugo Cloud, **The End of a World,** *1994, duraflex photograph, 14 x 11 inches. (Modernism Gallery, San Francisco)*

Just as absinthe symbolized the Bohemian decadence of Belle Époque Paris, the streamlined, high-octane Martini was a liquid icon for the American Dream. If you were drinking Martinis, you had either arrived or you were well on your way to where you were going. You didn't have to be a millionaire to like Martinis, either. The great alto sax player Paul Desmond of the Dave Brubeck Quartet was once asked how he developed his tart, lyrical style, and he replied, "I think I had it in the back of my mind that I wanted to sound like a dry martini."

"Who can visualize the world before 1860, a world in which the dry Martini had no place?" wrote J.A. Maxtone Graham in 1968, a decade when the Martini was at its zenith. "It must have been a bleak and arid earth that lacked the frosty, limpid, and luminous brew that today transforms the weary, work-laden executive into a sparkling and rejuvenated companion, or makes the child-bound housewife feel, for one evening hour, like a queen."

Like many pleasurable pastimes, Martini-drinking is bound in paradox. In spite of its shimmering diamond-like purity, the Martini can become a

"*I don't know anything about art, but this is a damned good Martini.*"

Drawing by Tobey; © *1956 The New Yorker Magazine, Inc.*

In 1951 a Martini competition was staged in Chicago. The winner was a Martini made with an anchovy-stuffed olive that was served in a glass rinsed with Cointreau. (Time/Life)

catalyst for uncivilized behavior, debauchery, and ruin when consumed to excess. The number of romances started by the drink probably equals those it has ended. As the redoubtable newspaper columnist of the forties, Westbrook Pegler, said, "More people get their glasses broken and arrested and divorced on account of martinis than for any other reason."

During the late seventies, America turned briefly away from the Martini. The days of the three-Martini lunch disappeared, thanks to Breathalyzer tests, changing health habits, and the demands of the work place. Yet in the late eighties the Martini made a strong comeback, particularly with the baby-boomer generation's shift in taste from gin to vodka. Bartenders across the country report that the Martini is once again the favorite mixed drink in America. Why?

Some bartenders say the Martini Revival reflects America's nostalgia for the fifties—diners, the classic Corvette, Elvis Presley music, Googie furniture, and old television sitcoms such as *I Love Lucy*. Faith Popcorn, guru of trend analysis and founder of the marketing firm BrainReserve Inc., explained in the *New York Times* that "the Martini may again be popular because self-indulgence has replaced self-denial as the reigning fashion."

I see it differently. Regardless of whether the Martini is a detriment or blessing to mankind, The Perfect Martini, as an idea, has infinite possibilities. For me, the Dry Martini remains an American symbol of elusive perfection, a kind of pagan Holy Grail. The dedicated Martini drinker views this deceptively simple cocktail as a true, if fleeting, salvation, a chance to savor the best possible moment before war, bankruptcy, or time itself takes it all away. A friend once told William F. Buckley, Jr., "When I get to St. Peter, I'm going to ask him to take me to the man who invented the dry martini. Because I just want to say, 'Thanks.'"

Just as some people speak of God while others say god(s), in this book I refer to the drink with a capital "M," unless I am quoting another source that uses lower-case spelling. As in religion, one may not have actually witnessed the Conception of the Perfect Martini, but one accepts on faith that it exists, and that it takest away the sins of the earth—at least until tomorrow's hangover. Whosoever shall believe in the Martini shall have salvation at cocktail hour.

"Then there was Perry's, where they made a wonderful martini for 15 cents, and when I say a martini and wonderful, you know it must have been good because there is the orneriest, meanest, no-damn-goodest mess of rancor ever concocted, and it causes more fights and more people get their glasses broken and arrested and divorced on account of martinis than for any other reason."
— **Westbrook Pegler**

Wayne Thiebaud,
Martini with Olive,
undated, oil on board,
9 1/4 x 7 3/4 inches,
signed upper right.
(Campbell-Thiebaud Gallery, San Francisco)

When I had nothing better to do in the old days in Chicago I used to amuse myself by thinking out new cocktails, but when you come down to brass-tacks there's nothing to beat a dry Martini. — W. Somerset Maugham, "The Fall of Edward Bannard," 1921

Chapter One

DUBIOUS ORIGINS

My INTEREST IN MARTINIS PROBABLY BEGAN IN CHILD-hood. During the fifties and sixties my father owned a saloon in San Francisco called El Matador, a swank place frequented by David Niven, Eva Gabor, and Tyrone Power who came for good jazz and cold Martinis. Though I drank ginger ale when I first sat at the bar as a ten-year-old, I heard magic in the gravel-like hiss of the Martini shaker. It went well with the jazz piano, the low lighting, and the conversational secrets of adult life. I wasn't cool then, but I knew Martinis were cool, and eventually I would drink them. And after all, the Martini was born in San Francisco, wasn't it?

Maybe not.

The history of most cocktails is clouded in myth, and the Martini is no exception. There are at least three American stories about the invention of the Martini.

During Prohibition, it took a special knock or the right name to get into a speakeasy.

Tyrone Power stepped behind the bar to share a Martini with the author's father at his famed San Francisco nightclub, El Matador, circa 1955. (Author's collection)

Many sources claim the drink was first named the *Martinez* by "Professor" Jerry Thomas, a legendary bartender. Call this The San Francisco Story. Born in New Haven, Connecticut in 1825, Thomas sailed around the Horn in 1849, reaching San Francisco at the height of the Gold Rush. As a barman at the El Dorado, Thomas became famous for inventing cocktails, and he dazzled customers by juggling a stream of flaming alcohol between a pair of solid silver mixing cups.

After a stint in New York, he returned to San Francisco and set up bar in the Occidental Hotel on Montgomery Street. As the story goes, a traveler on his way to the town of Martinez, California, stepped into the bar, threw a gold nugget on the table, and asked Thomas to shake up something special. "Very well, here is a new drink I have invented for your trip,"

Occidental Hotel, San Francisco, 1870s.

A thirsty California goldminer may have inspired the first Martinez cocktail. Daguerreotype, 1860.

said Thomas. "We'll call it the Martinez." No date has ever been attached to this propitious moment, and it was not even recorded in detail until 1927 when Herbert Asbury profiled Thomas for H.L. Mencken's *American Mercury*.

This makes a nice fable, but it isn't the whole story. What is verifiable is this: In 1862 the Professor published *The Bar-tender's Guide*, the first comprehensive manual for bartenders. It was an instant hit and enlarged his reputation. The Professor moved to New York in 1865 and established himself as one of the great bartenders of Gotham, inventing both the Tom & Jerry and the flaming Blue Blazer. He not only sponsored lively minstrel shows but gave the great political cartoonist Thomas Nast a first exhibition—in his saloon. His bartending book was reprinted several times, notably in an expanded last edition of 1887 that included twenty-four recipes, including the *Martinez*. The recipe read as follows:

Legendary barman "Professor" Jerry Thomas mixing a Blue Blazer.

> Use small bar glass
> One dash of bitters
> Two dashes of Maraschino
> One wineglass of vermouth
> Two small lumps of ice
> One pony of Old Tom gin
> **SHAKE** up thoroughly, and strain into a large cocktail glass.
> **Put a quarter of a slice of lemon in the glass, and serve.**
> *If the guest prefers it very sweet, add two dashes of gum syrup.*

This doesn't sound very much like the modern Martini. Despite the vestigial name, the Professor's almost candy like concoction was made

Bartender Martini di Arma di Taggia claimed to have invented the Martini at the Knickerbocker Hotel in New York in 1912.

with London gin, a sweetened product known as Old Tom, which no modern Dry Martini connoisseur would allow near the glass. More problematic is the fact that several reputable histories of the Martini have mistakenly reported that the 1887 edition of Thomas' book was similar to the 1862 version, hence leading to the conclusion that Thomas had invented the drink as early as 1862. However, the *Martinez* was not among his original ten recipes.

By the turn of the century, a flurry of American bar manuals contained a recipe for a drink called the *Martini* that had been simplified to just sweet vermouth and gin in equal parts with an optional dash of orange bitters.

As the Martini matured in popularity, its paternity was contested, giving rise to a second theory. Call this The Martinez Story. Citizens of Martinez, California, claimed that around 1870 a miner from San Francisco stopped his horse at Julio Richelieu's saloon on Ferry Street in Martinez for a bottle of whiskey. Richelieu was a young Frenchman who had come up to Contra Costa County from New Orleans. The miner plunked a tobacco sack of gold nuggets on the bar near the weigh-scales and handed Richelieu a bottle. The bartender filled the container with whiskey from a large barrel, but the traveler said he wasn't quite satisfied. To make up the difference, Richelieu picked up a glass, mixed him a small drink, and dropped an olive in it. "What is it?" asked the miner. "That," replied Richelieu, "is a Martinez cocktail."

Richelieu left Martinez to operate barrooms in San Francisco, his last saloon being Lotta's Fountain on the corner of Kearny and Market. Richelieu served a Free Lunch and a number of gourmet cocktails, but the Martinez was his specialty in the 1880s. Although Richelieu didn't stake his claim with a bar manual, the town of Martinez still insists that it is the Birthplace of the Martini; in 1992, a zealous group installed a brass plaque on the corner of Alhambra and Masonic to declare this "fact."

There were also European claims of authorship. An Italian connection surfaced in Martini di Arma di Taggia, an immigrant bartender at the

Jerry Kearns, Golden Gate, 1994, mixed media, 8 5/16 x 6 15/16 inches. (Modernism Gallery, San Francisco)

Knickerbocker Hotel in New York; he claimed that prior to the First World War he poured a drink that included dry gin, dry vermouth, and orange bitters. The story was corroborated by British mixologist John Doxat in his *World of Drinks and Drinking* (1971), who tape-recorded testimony from yet another ancient Italian bartender (the famous Luigi of the Savoia Majestic Hotel in Genoa) who recalled drinking Martini's Martini at the Knickerbocker in 1912. However, this late date already marks Signore di Arma di Taggia as a follower.

According to English lore, the drink's name derived from the Martini & Henry rifle used by the British army between 1871 and 1891. (The inventor of the big-bore man killer was actually a Swiss named Friedrich von Martini.) Both rifle and drink shared a strong kick. The

Martinez, California, claims to be the "Birthplace of the Martini."

Y

Oxford English Dictionary gives the earliest use of the word Martini as 1894, citing an advertisement for Heublein's Club Cocktails—a line of premixed drinks. But the *OED* erroneously states that "Martini" comes from Martini & Rossi vermouth, when that brand was not even imported into the United States at the time.

To complicate matters, early bartenders documented at least two other cocktails whose recipes resembled the modern Martini but which appeared under different names. In 1896, Thomas Stuart published a manual (*Stuart's Fancy Drinks and How to Mix Them*) in New York that gave a recipe for what he called the Marguerite Cocktail:

I dash of orange bitters
2/3 Plymouth gin
I/3 French vermouth

The Heublein Company has been marketing premixed Martinis since 1894.

Plymouth gin, unlike Old Tom, was not sweet; French vermouth was dry. And orange bitters has been cited as an ingredient of the classic Dry Martini up into the 1950s. This recipe, in my opinion, is the first documented modern Martini. (After the Martini itself went dry, the Marguerite evolved into a drink involving egg whites and lime juice.)

To make matters even more complicated, Martini sleuth Lowell Edmunds (author of *The Silver Bullet*, 1981) established that O.H. Byron included a Martinez recipe in his book *The Modern Bartender's Guide* of 1884—three years before Professor Jerry Thomas' book. And for the record, the first mention of the word Martini was in the *New and Improved Illustrated Bartender's Manual or How to Mix Drinks of the Present Style* published by Harry Johnson in 1888. But, as before, this recipe called for sweet gin, and Mr. Johnson roiled the waters of logic by sloppily labeling an illustration of the drink *Martine*.

In the long run, it may be impossible to decide who invented the Martini, but by 1900, the dawn of the Cocktail Age, the word Martini was in common usage among bartenders on both sides of the Atlantic.

We walked into the bar with that defiant feeling that characterizes the day of departure and ordered four Martinis. After one cocktail a change came over him—he suddenly reached across and slapped my knee with the first joviality I had seen him exhibit for months.   —   F. Scott Fitzgerald, "The Rich Boy," 1926

Chapter Two

THE SOCIAL CAREER OF A DRINK

Mark Stock, The Butler's In Love, 1994, oil on canvas, 24 x 18 inches. (Modernism Gallery, San Francisco)

GIN CAME TO AMERICA WITH THE FIRST DUTCH settlers, yet it trailed whiskey and brandy in popularity for the first hundred years of the Republic. By the end of the nineteenth century, there were about 1,600 registered trademarks for whiskey manufacturers in America, but only sixty for gin. (There were none for vermouth, since it was not yet manufactured in America.) The Martini was born at least a century ago, but its Golden Age begins in the twentieth century.

As early as 1904, O. Henry mentions the Martini in *The Gentle Grafter,* a comic tale in which Parley-voo Pickens and his partner, Caligula Polk,

Y

kidnap the wealthiest citizen of Mountain Valley, Georgia, and decide to treat him royally with a fancy meal:

So at twelve o'clock we had a hot lunch ready that looked like a banquet on a Mississippi River steamboat. We spread it on top of two or three big boxes, opened two quarts of the red wine, set the olives and a canned oyster cocktail and a ready-made Martini by the colonel's plate, and called him to grub.

Paul Iribe's 1931 print, **The Bad Genie,** *was part of a clever campaign to denigrate the invasion of France by American cocktails. It was sponsored by the powerful wine company, Nicolas.*

The episode tells us two things. Not only is the Martini so well-known at the dawn of the century that O. Henry can mention it without explanation, but a liquor company—in typical American fashion—has already marketed a ready-made version. (Indeed, the Heublein Company offered a premixed Martini as early as 1894.)

Cocktails, particularly those made with gin, were increasingly popular. The Martini's speedy ascent, begun during World War I, stalled during the first days of Prohibition and then, ironically, accelerated. But on January 16, 1920, thirty-six states ratified the Eighteenth Amendment to the Constitution and the selling of alcoholic beverages was forbidden by law. Bars

During Prohibition, revenue agents broke through a wall on Mulberry Street in New York City to find an illicit still.

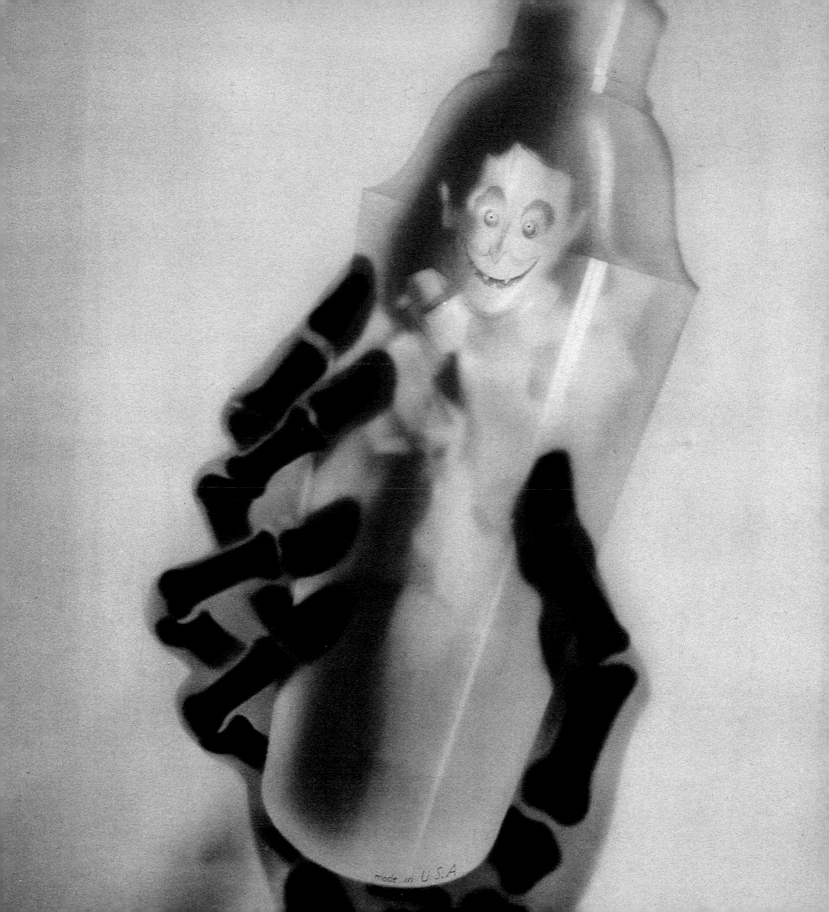

Two members of the Crusaders, an anti-Prohibition organization, display a fanciful map showing Chicago speakeasies in 1932.

Gerald Murphy, Cocktail, 1927, oil on canvas, 29 x 28 inches. A friend of Hemingway and Picasso, Murphy was a stylish expatriate in Paris who saw the American bar through a cubist vision. He was also the model for Dick Diver in Fitzgerald's Tender Is the Night. (Dallas Museum of Fine Arts)

and taverns from coast to coast closed their doors, but many reopened elsewhere as speakeasies. Bootleggers found it easier to make drinkable gin than whiskey, and bathtub gin became the liquid currency of the underworld. "Some speakeasies are disguised behind florists' shops, or behind undertakers' coffins," reported a French observer in New York. "I know one, right on Broadway, which is entered through an imitation telephone box." The 21 Club, then known as Jack and Charlie's, had a trick to beat a police raid: an emergency button would flip the bottles on the bar shelf down a chute to the basement.

Prohibition ruined the restaurant business in cities, and posh establishments such as New York's Delmonico's, which depended on wines and champagne, soon went out of business. And it changed the way Americans drank. While across the country general liquor consumption was down, city dwellers drank more per capita, and the trend was towards a mass binge on hard liquor.

Spanish surrealist filmmaker Luis Buñuel—an ardent Martini drinker—wrote in his 1982 memoir, *My Last Sigh:*

I never drank so much in my life as the time I spent five months in the United States during Prohibition. I had a two-fingered bootlegger friend in Los Angeles who taught me that the way to tell real gin from ersatz was to shake the bottle in a certain way. Real gin, he assured me, bubbles. It was a time when you could get your whiskey in the local pharmacy, with a prescription, and your wine in a coffee cup when you went to the right restaurant. . . . Prohibition was clearly one of the more nonsensical ideas of the century. Americans got fabulously drunk, although with repeal they seem to have learned to drink more intelligently.

Luis Buñuel

Until Prohibition ended in 1934, Americans had little access to high-proof, highly fragrant gins, but the cheap stuff was easy to make. "The gin is aged about the length of time it takes to get from the bathroom where it is made to the front porch where the cocktail party is in progress," claimed one bar book. So bartenders disguised bathtub gin

John Held, Jr.
ink drawing.
(Collection of
William Bliss)

with a "civilizing" dose of vermouth in a one-to-two ratio. The Martini cocktail was sipped from a small chilled glass with a twist of lemon.

Since Prohibition gin wasn't of the best quality, new cocktails were invented to mask the crude taste—especially for the ladies. A 1934 Martini & Rossi advertisement in *Vanity Fair* noted, "They're disappearing fast, thank goodness—those vicious liquid heartburns. People are going back to civilized cocktails—Martinis. . . ."

After signing the act repealing Prohibition, Franklin Roosevelt mixed the first legal Martini in the White House. Cocktails moved from the speakeasy to the legal bar and, finally, to the living room, where, along with

EXCERPT FROM
"FOR THE WAYWARD AND BEGUILED"
BY BERNARD DEVOTO

It does not matter in the least whether you shake a martini or stir it. It does matter if splinters of ice get into the cocktail glass, and I suppose this small seed of fact is what grew into the absurdity that we must not "bruise the gin." The gin will take all that you are capable of giving it, and so will the vermouth. An old hand will probably use a simple glass pitcher, as convenient and functional; it has no top and so cannot readily be shaken. But if a friend has given you a shaker, there are bar-strainers in the world and you need no ice-splinters in your martinis.

A martini, I repeat, is made of gin and vermouth. Dry vermouth. Besides many bad vermouths, French, Italian, and domestic, there are many good ones. With a devoted spirit keep looking for one that will go harmoniously with the gin of your choice and is dependably uniform in taste. You have found a friend: stay with it. Stay with them both, store them in quantity lest mischance or sudden want overtake you, and in a world of change you will be able to count on your martinis from season unto season, year to year. . . .

Sound practice begins with ice. There must be a lot of it, much more than the catechumen dreams, so much that the gin smokes when you pour it in. A friend of mine has said it for all time; his formula ends, "and five hundred pounds of ice." Fill the pitcher with ice, whirl it till dew forms on the glass, pour out the melt, put in another handful of ice. Then as swiftly as possible pour in the gin and vermouth, at once bring the mixture as close to freezing point of alcohol as can be reached outside the laboratory and pour out the martinis. You must be unhurried but you must work fast, for a diluted martini would be a contradiction in terms, a violation of nature's order. That is why the art requires so much ice and why the artist will never mix more than a single round at a time, counting noses. . . .

There is a point where the marriage of gin and vermouth is consummated. It varies a little with the constituents, but for a gin of 95 proof and a harmonious vermouth it may be generalized as about 3.7 to one. And that is not only the proper proportion but the critical one; if you use less gin it is a marriage in name only and the name is not martini. You get a drinkable and even pleasurable result, but not art's sunburst of imagined delight becoming real. Happily, the upper limit is not so fixed; you may make it four to one or a little more than that, which is a comfort if you cannot do fractions in your head and an assurance when you must use an unfamilar gin. But not much more. This is the violet hour, the hour of hush and wonder, when the affections glow again and valor is reborn, when the shadows deepen magically along the edge of the forest and we believe that, if we watch carefully, at any moment we see the unicorn. But it would not be a martini if we should see him.

(*Harper's*, December 1949)

listening to the radio, the cocktail hour became an American institution. London gin was now being made in places such as Peoria, Illinois, and even Modesto, California, was producing vermouth.

By the forties, the gin in the Martini grew dominant, with proportions of three or four parts gin to one part vermouth. The less vermouth, the "drier" the Martini. Robert Benchley's solution to almost any problem was gin and "just enough vermouth to take away that nasty, watery look." There were drinkers so fastidious about dryness that they merely coated the shaker with vermouth, then poured it off—a method called

Patrons of the Greenwich Village Inn celebrated the return of stand-up drinking of hard liquor in New York City in May, 1934.

"in and out." Fanatics went further: Sir Winston Churchill, by his own account, made Martinis by pouring gin into a pitcher and glancing briefly at a bottle of vermouth across the room.

The Martini rode a wave of American dynamism during World War II that crested in the post-war affluence of the fifties. Now familarly known as a Silver Bullet or See-through, the Martini became a symbol of the up-per-middle class. The man who had *arrived* needed a drink appropriate to his new status. In her poem "Cinderella," Anne Sexton described a milk-man who had made an overnight fortune in real estate turning "from ho-mogenized to Martinis at lunch."

There was a down side to the fad. As C.B. Palmer wrote of the fifties, "In New York, however, the affliction that is cutting down the productive time in the office and destroying the benign temper of most of the bar-tenders is the thing called the *very* dry martini. It is a mass madness, a cult, a frenzy, a body of folklore, a mystique, an *expertise* of a sort which may well earn for this decade the name of the Numb (or Glazed) Fifties. . . . Along every stretch of polished mahogany in public places and in countless liv-ing rooms there is no talk of the world crisis or of [presidential candidate

Sir Winston Churchill made Martinis by pouring gin into a pitcher and glancing briefly at a bottle of vermouth across the room.

The first legal gin shipment left Philadelphia for San Francisco on October 23, 1933— with a stylish stowaway in the cargo.

Estes] Kefauver's chances but only of how to get a martini *really* dry."

In the sixties Tom Lehrer sang, "Hearts full of youth, hearts full of truth / Six parts gin to one part vermouth." It was a decade that produced a number of gadgets to satisfy this obsession for dryness. There was Gorham's Martini spike (a large silver syringe) and Invento's large dropper for dispensing vermouth in precise amounts. There was also a vermouth

EXCERPT FROM
"TO THE GIBSON AND BEYOND"
BY M.F.K. FISHER

The first Martini I ever drank was strictly medicinal, for threatened seasickness, and in spite of a loyal enjoyment of them which may be increasing in direct ratio to my dwindling selectivity of palate, I must admit that I still find them a sure prop to my flagging spirits, my tired or queasy body, even my over-timid social self. I think I know how many to drink, and when, and where, as well as why: and if I have acted properly and heeded all my physical and mental reactions to them, I have been the winner in many an otherwise lost bout with everything from boredom to plain funk. A well-made dry Martini or Gibson, correctly chilled and nicely served, has been more often my true friend than any two-legged creature.

The tipple, however, can be dangerous. When about to drink one, I make sure of several things, but mainly how soon I can expect to sit down to a bite to eat. If things look as if they would drift on; if my host has a glint of pre-dinner wanderings and droppings-in in his eye; if my hostess seems disarmingly vague about how to get a meal on the table; if all this obtrudes no matter how quietly into my general enthusiasm, I say No to no matter how masterly a mixture of gin, vermouth, and lemon-zest.

If, on the other hand, I see plainly that I can relax, confident of tangible nourishment within the hour, I permit myself the real pleasure of a definite alcoholic wallop. (*Atlantic Monthly*, January 1949)

atomizer for spraying the inside of the shaker. In a 1968 issue of *Gourmet*, J.A. Maxtone Graham noted a strange experiment:

> *Two years ago in Chicago an attempt was made to classify tastes in Martinis. A dreadful-sounding machine called a MartiniMatic enabled 3,426 random people to dial a drink of their chosen strength. Marked differences in blend were shown according to professions: teachers, factory workers, and office workers chose 3 to 1; salesmen, buyers, and engineers chose 4 to 1; admen chose 5 to 1; and publishers chose 7 to 1.*

Gordon's Gin advertisement, 1951. The label is distinguished by a border of juniper berries, an essential ingredient in gin.

George Jean Nathan, the well-known New York drama critic of the 20s, was reputed to have an ingenious device rigged up in his apartment. A series of strings and pulleys attached his front-door latch to his refrigerator, so that when he turned the key to enter, the cocktail shaker in the refrigerator was gently agitated and the martini within it was ready for consumption by the time he reached the kitchen.

The bar at the Central Park Casino in 1936.

There were more bizarre inventions. Using rubber gloves and a thermos of minus 400 degrees Fahrenheit liquid nitrogen, one experimenter invented a Martini-Sicle, which was sucked on the end of a stick. The Pennsylvania candy company of John Wagner and Sons, Inc. combined all the herbal ingredients of a Martini into a sweet candy called The Dry Martini. Its box depicted a smiling Eskimo and a chummy polar bear hoisting Martini glasses at the North Pole.

These candies tasted like a Martini without the alcohol.

Even Ernest Hemingway had his methods for achieving coldness well and true, writing in a letter to a friend:

We have found a way of making ice in the deep freeze in tennis ball tubes that comes out 15 degrees below zero and with glasses frozen too makes the coldest martini in the world. Just enough vermouth to cover the bottom of the glass, ³/4 ounce of gin, and the Spanish cocktail onions very crisp and also 14 degrees below zero when they go into the glass.

A classic gin Martini with olive, accompanied by a silver dish by William Spratling and a 1936 penguin shaker by Napier. (John William Lund photograph)

The strain he was under was terrific. . . . By the end of the day he was exhausted, and, as never before, he sought relief behind the wall of alcoholic inhibition. Straight to his hotel he was driven, and straight to his rooms he went, where immediately was mixed for him the first of a series of double martinis. — **Jack London,** **Burning Daylight,** *1910*

Chapter Three

The Martini in Literature and Film

Jack London was the first major American novelist to use the Martini as a symbol for power. Elam Harnish, the hero of his novel *Burning Daylight*, is a man of action who makes millions in the 1898 Yukon Gold Rush, then becomes a tycoon in San Francisco. In the process, he switches from rotgut whiskey to fancy cocktails, drinking to relieve the pressure of success. He rapidly goes downhill.

London himself had a gargantuan appetite for alcohol (which killed him at age 40) but never mixed his own cocktails. A San Francisco bartender would mix up huge quantities of Martinis and ship them up to Wolf House, the author's hideaway in Sonoma's Valley of the Moon.

Jack London

Ernest Hemingway and Marlene Dietrich shared Martinis and a soulful glance at the Stork Club in 1946. Hemingway liked his Martinis very cold and served with an olive. Dietrich liked men who liked Martinis.

By the early twentieth century, the American vogue for cocktails moved to Europe where *le bar américain* was the latest rage. In the cafés of Toulouse-Lautrec's Paris and in the London clubs of Evelyn Waugh, the Martini became known as a Gin and French or Gin 'n' It. When Hemingway's young hero and alter ego Frederic Henry in *A Farewell to Arms* (1929) separates himself from the barbaric suffering of World War I, he knows exactly how to put his troubles aside. He joins his lover Catherine Barkley at the Grand-Hôtel & des Iles Borromées and heads to the bar. "The sandwiches came and I ate three and drank a couple more martinis," he says. "I had never tasted anything so cool and clean. They made me feel civilized."

During Prohibition (1920–1934), Americans had to go abroad to drink openly. A 1926 novel by John Thomas, *Dry Martini: A Gentleman Turns to Love*, recounted the life of an American expatriate, Willoughby Quimby,

EXCERPT FROM
THE SUN ALSO RISES
BY ERNEST HEMINGWAY

We touched the two glasses as they stood side by side on the bar. They were coldly beaded. Outside the curtained window was the summer heat of Madrid.

"I like an olive in a Martini," I said to the barman.

"Right you are, sir. There you are."

"Thanks."

"I should have asked, you know."

The barman went far enough up the bar so that he would not hear our conversation. Brett had sipped from the Martini as it stood, on the wood. Then she picked it up. Her hand was steady enough to lift it after that first sip.

"It's good. Isn't it a nice bar?"

"They're all nice bars."

"You know I didn't believe it at first. He was born in 1905. I was in school in Paris, then. Think of that."

"Anything you want me to think about it?"

"Don't be an ass. *Would* you buy a lady a drink?"

"We'll have two more Martinis."

"As they were before, sir?"

"They were very good." Brett smiled at him.

"Thank you, ma'am."

"Well, bung-o," Brett said.

"Bung-o!"

"You know," Brett said, "he'd only been with two women before. He never cared about anything but bullfighting."

"He's got plenty of time."

"I don't know. He thinks it was me. Not the show in general."

"Well, it was you."

"Yes. It was me."

"I thought you weren't going to ever talk about it."

"How can I help it?"

"You'll lose it if you talk about it."

"I just talk around it. You know I feel rather damned good, Jake."

"You should."

"You know it makes one feel rather good deciding not to be a bitch."

"Yes."

"It's sort of what we have instead of God."

"Some people have God," I said. "Quite a lot."

"He never worked very well for me."

"Should we have another Martini?"

The barman shook up two more Martinis and poured them into fresh glasses.

who lives a dissolute gentleman's existence in Paris. Quimby has a mistress and has not seen his daughter in years; when they are reunited, he falls hopelessly in love with her young traveling companion. Then his ex-wife reappears and he falls in love with her as well, only to learn that she plans to marry someone else. At the book's conclusion, Quimby is as alone as he was at the beginning. Recaged in his "prison of liberty" he does the only logical thing. He heads back to "Dan's place," that is, the bar at the Ritz:

"Dry Martini, please, Dan," said Willougby Quimby as he placed a contented foot upon the rail.

David Niven sneaks a Martini in **My Man Godfrey**, *1957.*

The great sage of Martini lore is Lowell Edmunds, head of the Classics department at Rutgers University. In his scholarly treatise, *The Silver Bullet* (1981), Edmunds noted the ritual aspect of Martini-drinking. First is the communal Martini, which might be shared at a bar with business associates, at a club with friends, or in a family setting. "The Martini is in each case the totem-drink that binds together the members of the tribe," he posits. "Accordingly, the mixing of the Martini is a rite, whether performed by the host or by the bartender, either of whom may assume the role of the priest."

Drawing by Claude;
© 1959, 1987 The New
Yorker Magazine, Inc.

For gin, in cruel
Sober truth,
Supplies the fuel
For flaming youth.
—**Noel Coward**

The opposite category is the solo Martini drinker—a self-contained but stable traveler who imbibes a reasonable number of Martinis without crossing the line into maudlin drunkenness. As M.F.K. Fisher confessed proudly, "A well-made Martini or Gibson, correctly chilled and nicely served, has been more often my true friend than any two-legged creature." (A Gibson is simply a Martini with a pickled onion instead of lemon twist or olive.)

Of course, sitting a few stools down the bar one might find the antisocial loner on the way to alcoholism. "This isolating Martini is potentially, perhaps even essentially, uncivilized," writes Edmunds. "The civilized antidote to civilization seems especially prone to misuse when it is taken in seclusion, apart from society, and that is because the Martini always carries with it the possibility of excess."

Ernest Hemingway drank Martinis from Paris and Venice to New York and Key West. During the Liberation of Paris in 1944, Hemingway led two truckloads of grubby Free French soldiers into the Ritz Hotel, that citadel of world-class luxury. In the Ritz's deserted lobby they found only one person, a frightened assistant manager. With relief he recognized

Martini & Rossi
advertisement, 1954.

For a dry aperitif
DRY
MARTINI
better drink
MARTINI
vermouth

Hemingway as a frequent prewar guest and asked if he could be of service. Hemingway looked back at his jubilant, scruffy horde and answered, "How about seventy-three dry martinis?"

If the Martini taken in lonely isolation symbolizes dashed dreams inexpressible even to a sympathetic bartender, then the Martini shared with friends represents future happiness, prosperity, and romance. When a man and woman clink glasses and whisper, "Here's to us," the Martini may function ritualistically as an aphrodisiac.

In Hemingway's novel, *Across the River and into the Trees*, the aging hero, Colonel Cantwell, meets his nineteen-year-old Italian sweetheart at Harry's Bar in Venice:

> *"Waiter," the Colonel called; then asked, "Do you want a dry Martini, too?"*
> *"Yes," she said. "I'd love one."*
> *"Two very dry Martinis," the Colonel said.*
> *"Montgomerys. Fifteen to one."*
> *The waiter, who had been in the desert, smiled and was gone, and the Colonel turned to Renata.*
> *"You're nice," he said. "You're also very beautiful and lovely and I love you."*

Hemingway called them Montgomerys for the British general; it was said that in his desert campaigns of World War II, Monty would only attack the Germans' Afrika Corps if his troops outnumbered them by a fifteen-to-one ratio. Hemingway's aging but amorous colonel seems to have the advantage over the young, eager Venetian:

> *"Then let us have another Martini," the girl said. "You know I never drank a Martini until we met."*
> *"I know. But you drink them awfully well."*

Implicit in the scene is a feminine submission to a male-initiated rite. Hemingway's Martini courtship culminates in a murky scene in which the

Humphrey Bogart's last words supposedly were: "I should never have switched from Scotch to Martinis."

This fanciful 1950s advertisement was done by Andy Warhol in his pre-Pop days.

colonel and the young woman make love in the privacy of a boat cruising the canals of Venice.

Martinis also appear in John Dos Passos' *Manhattan Transfer* and in short stories by John Cheever. In the classic tale "The Five Forty-Eight," Cheever's spineless businessman, Blake, has had an affair with his mentally unstable secretary and then fires her. Intent on revenge, she suddenly appears on a rainy day and pursues him down Madison Avenue, forcing him to take refuge in a men's bar:

> *He ordered a Gibson and shouldered his way in between two other men at the bar, so that if she should be watching him from the window she would lose sight of him. The place was crowded with commuters putting down a drink before the ride home. They had brought in on their clothes—on their shoes and umbrellas—the rancid smell of the wet dusk outside, but Blake began to relax as soon as he tasted his Gibson and looked around at the common, mostly not-young faces that surrounded him and that were worried, if they worried at all, about tax rates and who would be put in charge of merchandising.*

Edward Ruscha, Sin *(with an Olive), 1970, silkscreen, edition of 150, 19 x 26 ¹/₂ inches. (Modernism Gallery, San Francisco)*

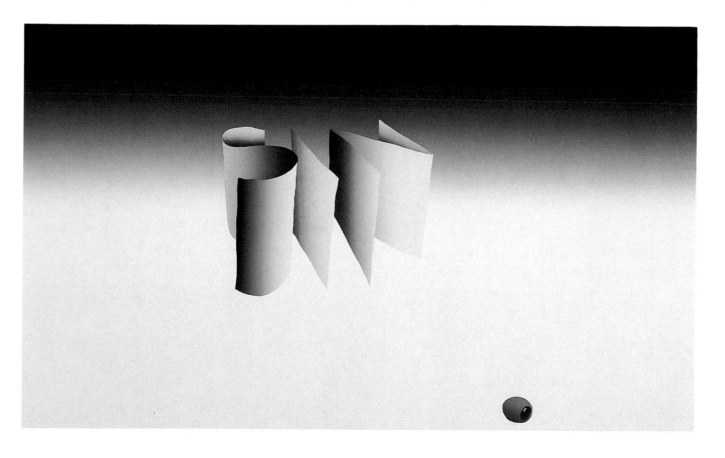

Eventually the troubled woman corners Blake on the commuter train, thrusts a pistol against his Brooks Brothers raincoat, and forces him off the train at an empty station where she humiliates him.

The Martini is an adult drink. In the first act of the musical *Mame*, Auntie Mame's precocious ten-year-old nephew, Patrick, pops into the living room to greet the stuffy bank trustee Mr. Babcock, and disarms him by asking, "Would you care for a Martini, Mr. Babcock?" The guest protests, but Patrick insists, saying that it won't hurt to imbibe a little early in the day, because "Mr. Woolcott says somewhere in the world the sun is always just below the yardarm." The funny part of the scene is watching a boy still in shorts as he mixes the manly Martini for the uptight banker. "Would you care for an olive? Auntie Mame says olives take up too much room in a little glass."

Willard Waterman and Rosalind Russell share Martinis in the film **Auntie Mame, 1958.**

Of course, when Mame enters the room, she finds Babcock holding the Martini and asks "if it makes the best first impression on a sensitive young mind to see you drinking in business hours."

"But he—" protests Babcock.

"Don't worry. I won't breathe a word to the Knickerbocker Bank."

EXCERPT FROM
CASINO ROYALE
BY IAN FLEMING

When Bond rose, he too pushed back his chair and called cheerfully across the table:

"Thanks for the ride. Guess I owe you a drink. Will you join me?"

Bond had the feeling that this might be the C.I.A. man. He knew he was right as they strolled off together towards the bar, after Bond had thrown a plaque of ten mille to the croupier and had given a mille to the "huissier" who drew back his chair.

"My name's Felix Leiter," said the American. "Glad to meet you."

"Mine's Bond—James Bond."

"Oh, yes," said his companion, "and now let's see. What shall we have to celebrate?"

Bond insisted on ordering Leiter's Haig-and-Haig "on the rocks" and then he looked carefully at the barman.

"A dry martini," he said. "One. In a deep champagne goblet."

"Oui, monsieur."

"Just a moment. Three measures of Gordon's, one of vodka, half a measure of Kina Lillet. Shake it very well until it's ice-cold, then add a large thin slice of lemon-peel. Got it?"

"Certainly, monsieur." The barman seemed pleased with the idea.

"Gosh, that's certainly a drink," said Leiter.

Bond laughed. "When I'm . . . er . . . concentrating," he explained, "I never have more than one drink before dinner. But I do like that one to be large and very strong and very cold and very well-made. I hate small portions of anything, particularly when they taste bad. This drink's my own invention. I'm going to patent it when I can think of a good name."

He watched carefully as the deep glass became frosted with the pale golden drink, slightly aerated by the bruising of the shaker. He reached for it and took a long sip.

"Excellent," he said to the barman, "but if you can get a vodka made with grain instead of potatoes, you will find it still better."

"Mais n'enculons pas des mouches," he added in an aside to the barman. The barman grinned.

"That's a vulgar way of saying 'we won't split hairs,'" explained Bond.

Sean Connery as James Bond in Dr. No, *1962.*

"Now just one minute, where did this boy learn to mix—"

"Mr. Babcock," replies Mame. "Knowledge is power."

Naturally, the hero of John Leonard's 1964 novel *The Naked Martini* drinks them. Brian Kelly is an upwardly-mobile Irish boy on scholarship at Harvard whose roommate, Comstock, is old-line WASP fresh out of St. Mark's. "Kelly!" exclaims Comstock. "What can you do with a name like that? Strictly shantytown." Nonetheless, they become friends, and in Pygmalion tradition, Comstock takes Kelly under his wing, showing him how to select the right tweed suit, button-down shirts, and loafers. Kelly quickly "let his crew cut grow away, and learned to mix a mean martini." Soon Comstock introduces Kelly to a blond beauty from an old Harvard family, Elizabeth Kirkland. Kelly comes to think of her as a Martini Girl: "Pure chaste, cold steel, silver ice-pick-ish, blue Scandinavian pools."

After Brian has gone into advertising, Elizabeth invites him to her parents' house in Connecticut. On the train from Manhattan the humbly born Kelly contemplates the delights he will soon savor: "Liz was coming home. And he was invited for the weekend to the great rambling Stamford house, a place of low porches drooping over the Sound, scrag-

"*It was a very bleak period in my life, Louie. Martinis didn't help. Religion didn't help. Psychiatry didn't help. Transcendental meditation didn't help. Yoga didn't help. But Martinis helped a little.*"

Drawing by H. Martin; © 1975 The New Yorker Magazine, Inc.

gly rose gardens and tall hedges and charcoal-faced servants spilling martinis out of silver penguin pitchers."

Mrs. Kirkland greets him warmly, but when she asks, "How are you?" he makes a *faux-pas*, saying, "I've been anticipating one of your martinis all the way up from New York." The hostess frowns. "I'm so sorry. I thought Elizabeth had written you all about it. No martinis this evening, I'm afraid. This is a wine-tasting party."

Though Elizabeth openly offers herself to him, the evening goes badly and he realizes he does not fit into the world of the WASP—a tribe armored but also trapped by their own history and customs, a hegemony

Joan Crawford preferred her Martinis stirred not shaken in the MGM film **Humoresque, 1946.**

swiftly giving way to newcomers. The dream of the Martini is laid bare—
naked as the wanton Elizabeth herself. The Martini Girl is no longer cold,
chaste, and unattainable. The Martini as concept has been stripped down
to just lukewarm gin and unsavory vermouth. Kelly flees back to New York

where a self-made man, even one who went to Harvard on scholarship, won't feel like a freak of social engineering.

Drinking Martinis was a pastime of privilege, whether status was inherited or self-created. Take Dashiell Hammett's *The Thin Man*, starring William Powell as Nick Charles, a suave private eye whose favorite drink is the Martini. Hammett's novel did not mention the word Martini, but the film version was shot just as Prohibition ended, and the director made sure that when debonair Nick first appears on camera, he is in the elegant Normandie Hotel bar instructing three bartenders in the art of mixing Martinis. He tells them, "You see, the important thing is the rhythm. You always have rhythm in your shaking. With a Manhattan you shake to foxtrot time. A Bronx to two-step time. A dry Martini you always shake to waltz time."

When not tailing suspects, Nora (Myrna Loy) and Nick (William Powell) drink constantly in **The Thin Man.** *Nora watches with mild disgust as Nick shoots balloons off the Christmas tree.*

When Myrna Loy enters and finds him half-crocked, she orders six Martinis to catch up. Later while suffering from a hangover, she pulls aside the ice pack on her brow to ask, "What hit me?" And Nick replies, "The last Martini." After two centuries the gin once swilled in the slums of London and the speakeasies of America was being gracefully consumed in top hotels and in the salons of European nobility and Hollywood movie stars.

In my introduction I wrote that Robert Benchley said, "I must get out of these wet clothes and into a dry Martini." I said that to keep things simple, but informed sources tell me that there is more to the story. First, the quote is often misattributed to Alexander Woollcott, another wit from the Algonquin's Roundtable. (*Bartlett's Quotations* cited him in 1968.) In his 1944 book, *Try and Stop Me*, Bennet Cerf recounted an anecdote about Benchley coming in from a driving rain and delivering the immortal line. According to Benchley's son Nathaniel, "Robert never said, 'Let's get out of these wet clothes and into a dry martini,' although there are people who

"What hit me?" asks Nora after six Martinis. "The last Martini," Nick replies. Asta, the dog, commiserates.

will swear they were there when he said it. It was a joke in somebody's column, and a press agent picked it up and attributed it to Robert, and it stuck." The most reliable explanation I found was in Ralph Keyes' book *"Nice Guys Finish Seventh"* (1992). Keyes says that in the 1942, film *The Major and the Minor*, Benchley told Ginger Rogers, "Why don't you get out of that wet coat and into a dry martini?" The film was written by Charles Brackett (*Sunset Boulevard*) and Billy Wilder (who also directed).

Recently, veteran *Los Angeles Times* columnist Jack Smith asked Billy Wilder about the origin of the Martini line. The director said Benchley told him that the line had originated with his friend Charles Butterworth who actually said it after falling into the pool at the Garden of Allah (a fabled Hollywood resort). Smith figured he'd closed the case, until a reader wrote saying that a 1937 film called *Every Day's a Holiday* featured the following exchange between Butterworth and Charles Winninger:

Winninger (in wet evening clothes): *"I'm hot. Soaked all over."*
Butterworth: *"You ought to get out of those wet clothes and into a dry martini."*

Charles Butterworth probably was the first to say, "You ought to get out of those wet clothes and into a dry martini."

Charles Butterworth, Mae West, and Charles Winninger in Every Day's a Holiday, *1937.*

Mae West, who also starred in the film, got screenwriting credit. So maybe she wrote it? The *Oxford Dictionary of Modern Quotations* includes it under her name, and Jack Smith places his bet on her, but Ralph Keyes conjectured, "West was a notorious credit hog who hated to share billing with anyone, no matter how many of her lines they may have written."

(I favor Charlie Butterworth. A charmingly wimpy character actor of the thirties and forties, Charlie and my uncle Hunt were sailing to Hawaii aboard the *S.S. Lurline* and were well into their Martinis when they had a brilliant idea: they went up and down the stateroom corridors, picked up all the shoes that the passengers had put outside their doors to be polished, and tossed them overboard!)

John Register, Hollywood, 1989, silkscreen, edition of 75, 21 x 17 inches. The image appeared on the cover of Charles Bukowski's novel, Hollywood. *(Modernism Gallery, San Francisco)*

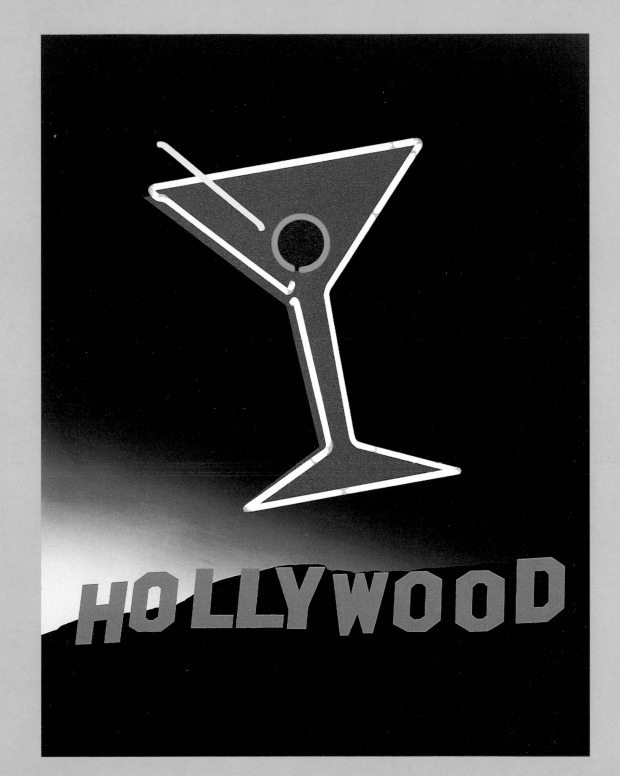

The Gibson is a Martini traditionally made with Old Tom or Dutch gin and garnished with an onion. It may have been named for Charles Dana Gibson, the artist who drew "the Gibson girl."

In *All About Eve* (1950) an aging Broadway actress named Margo Channing (Bette Davis) turns to Martinis when she realizes her ambitious young protégée Eve (Anne Baxter) is copying her every move and angling for her fiancé to boot. "I'd like a Martini, very dry," Margo says, adding that "the kid" might like a milkshake. But Eve is a quick study, and knows what a star orders. "A Martini, very dry, please." As guests arrive at the party, Davis swallows her Martini swiftly, and issues one of the great lines in cinematic bitchdom: "Fasten your seatbelts. It's going to be a bumpy ride."

Director Tony Brand tells me that some older directors still shout, "It's the Martini shot!" when they shoot the last scene of the day. In *The Fifty-Year Decline and Fall of Hollywood*, Ezra Goodman wrote that the young

Bette Davis drank too many Martinis with Thelma Ritter in All About Eve, 1950.

W.C. Fields drank Martinis for breakfast and consumed about two quarts of gin a day. He paid for it through his nose.

William Holden had a bar in his dressing room.

William Holden was the only film actor allowed by his teetotaling boss, Y. Frank Freeman, to have a bar in his dressing room. Holden used to say to his stand-in, "Warm up the ice-cubes," which was code for "mix me a drink." According to Goodman, in an experimental moment Holden once set fire to a Dry Martini and dubbed it a "Hot Martini."

In his later years W.C. Fields started the day with two double Martinis—"angel's milk," he called them—before breakfast. Then he put down a glass of pineapple juice, a piece of toast, and another Martini. He took an outsized cocktail shaker full of Martinis to the studio for the day's shoot. Lunch was crab meat salad and Martinis. In his biography of Fields, Robert Lewis Taylor estimated the actor drank about two quarts of gin a day. Late in the evening he would perform a trick of balancing a full Martini glass on his head. If the glass trembled, he said, "There, I've had a sufficiency." His skill and self-command were such that the glass rarely shook, and he then rewarded himself by emptying the contents.

Spanish surrealist Luis Buñuel was a great devoté of the Martini, and in *The Discreet Charm of the Bourgeoisie* (1972) he wrote a scene rife with snobbery. François and Raphael, one a French businessman, the other a suave,

Benny Goodman, the "King of Swing" was one of many celebrities to appear in Smirnoff's eye-catching ad campaign of the 1960s.

BENNY GOODMAN, WORLD-RENOWNED KING OF SWING

"IT LEAVES YOU BREATHLESS!" says Benny Goodman

Smooth, flawless Smirnoff gives you everything you ask for in a vodka. And nothing you *don't* want! Having virtually no taste of its own, it never "takes over" in your drinks. It has no "breath"... leaves no whisper of liquor on your lips. Let nobody tell you all vodkas are the same. Make sure you get the one and only *Smirnoff*. Just mention our name!

the vodka of vodkas

Smirnoff
THE GREATEST NAME IN VODKA

80 AND 100 PROOF. DISTILLED FROM GRAIN. STE. PIERRE SMIRNOFF FLS. (DIVISION OF HEUBLEIN), HARTFORD, CONN.

drug-dealing ambassador from an unnamed South American country, are preparing cocktails for their attractive women.

François: "Dry Martinis for everyone? There's no better tranquilizer. I read it in a woman's magazine. Let me do it. I'll mix it. These glasses aren't right. Styles have changed. For the dry Martini the ideal is a cone-shaped glass. Raphael knows that a dry Martini, like champagne, must be sipped and savored. We'll do a little experiment. Call in your chauffeur."

Raphael: "What do you want with my chauffeur?"

François: "You'll see."

The chauffeur, Maurice, enters. They offer him a Martini. He smiles and knocks it back in one gulp. After he leaves, François says, "See that? That's what shouldn't be done with a dry Martini."

His wife says, "Don't be nasty. Maurice is a commoner. He's not educated."

Raphael just shrugs. "No system can help the masses to acquire refinement. You know me. I'm not reactionary."

The Martini is composed of opposites: the brute strength of gin and the aromatic sensitivity of vermouth. Ian Fleming's spy, James Bond, was the human embodiment of the Martini. Bond was reckless with his women and rough on enemy agents, but extremely precise about his cocktail, asking it to be "large and very strong and very well made." In *Casino Royale* Bond tells the beautiful double agent, Vesper Lynd, about his special Martini made with gin and vodka and is suddenly inspired to name it for her. "The Vesper," he said. "It sounds perfect and it's very appropriate to the violet hour when my cocktail will now be drunk all over the world."

Sean Connery in **Goldfinger,** *1964. Williams Grimes said of Bond: "The first Transatlantic man, he is perfectly at home with advanced technology, flashy gadgetry, and foreign languages. The contrast with postwar Britain could not be more stark. . . . With his vodka martini, Bond announces, in effect, 'I am modern, therefore American.'"*

Did Fleming mean the gin and vodka to have symbolic rapport with the double agent? After all, vodka is Russian, and the girl works for them. After Vesper commits suicide, Bond never imbibes the gin and vodka Martini again. In later books he drinks everything from Bourbon to champagne, but in most of the films, beginning with *Dr. No* and *Goldfinger*, Bond drank a Martini, thus popularizing the expression "Shaken, not stirred."

Harpo Marx sounds off in this Smirnoff ad, 1961. Vodka began to overtake gin sales in the following decades.

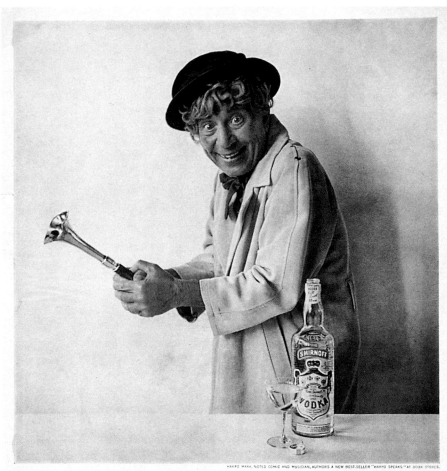

WHEN I HONK FOR VODKA, I EXPECT SMIRNOFF' Harpo, the silent one, may be excused from naming his brand. But you, gentle reader, should be specific. For, ever since Smirnoff changed the drinking habits of America, countless Johnny-come-lately vodkas have gotten into the act. To assure yourself of the flawless original, always call for your Smirnoff by name. It makes the driest Martinis, the smoothest Screwdrivers, the most delicious drinks of every kind. So know what you drink—drink what you know!

it leaves you breathless

Smirnoff®
THE GREATEST NAME IN VODKA

80 AND 100 PROOF. DISTILLED FROM GRAIN. ©STE. PIERRE SMIRNOFF FLS. (DIVISION OF HEUBLEIN), HARTFORD, CONN., 1961

Curiously, I never drink wine in a bar, for wine is a purely physical pleasure and does nothing to stimulate the imagination.

To provoke, or sustain, a reverie in a bar, you have to drink English gin, especially in the form of a dry martini. To be frank, given the primordial role played in my life by the dry martini, I think I really ought to give it at least a page. Like all cocktails, the martini, composed essentially of gin and a few drops of Noilly Prat, seems to have been an American invention. Connoisseurs who like their martinis very dry suggest simply allowing a ray of sunlight to shine through a bottle of Noilly Prat before it hits the bottle of gin. At a certain period in America it was said that the making of a dry martini should resemble the Immaculate Conception, for, as Saint Thomas Aquinas once noted, the generative power of the Holy Ghost pierced the Virgin's hymen "like a ray of sunlight through a window—leaving it unbroken."

Another crucial recommendation is that the ice be so cold and hard that it won't melt, since nothing's worse than a watery martini. For those who are still with me, let me give you my personal recipe, the fruit of long experimentation and guaranteed to produce perfect results. The day before your guests arrive, put all the ingredients—glasses, gin, and shaker—in the refrigerator. Use a thermometer to make sure the ice is about twenty degrees below zero (centigrade). Don't take anything out until your friends arrive; then pour a few drops of Noilly Prat and half a demitasse spoon of Angostura bitters over ice. Shake it, then pour it out, keeping only the ice, which retains a faint taste of both. Then pour straight gin over the ice, shake it again, and serve.

(During the 1940s, the director of the Museum of Modern Art in New York taught me a curious variation. Instead of Angostura, he used a dash of Pernod. Frankly, it seemed heretical to me, but apparently it was only a fad.)

As for the famous three-Martini lunch, I don't care how many Martinis anyone has with lunch, but I am concerned about who picks up the check. — **President Jimmy Carter, The New York Times, February 18, 1978**

Chapter Four

THE MARTINI AND POLITICS

FRANKLIN ROOSEVELT WAS AN ENTHUSIASTIC BUT unpredictable Martini-mixer. He served a Martini to Stalin at the 1943 Teheran Conference and asked how he liked it. "Well, all right," the Russian dictator replied, "but it is cold on the stomach." Roosevelt's usual recipe, as provided by his secretary to a nosy radio reporter named Jack Reed, was two parts gin to one part vermouth, with a teaspoon of olive brine. Although the FDR Martini was served with an olive, the rim of the glass was rubbed with lemon peel.

Stalin and FDR at the Teheran Conference, 1943.

One administration official characterized U.S.–Soviet relations under FDR as the "four martinis and let's have an agreement" era. Seventy-five-year-old Susan Mary Alsop recently recalled a visit to the Roosevelt White House: "They'd show you up and there was the president in that upstairs study shaking up dry martinis, which I adored. There would be what he called 'Uncle Joe's Bounty,' a large bowl of fresh caviar sent by Stalin.'"

Franklin D. Roosevelt drinking and smoking at the Mayflower Hotel.

FDR used this silver cocktail shaker to mix Martinis haphazardly but with great enthusiasm.

FDR mixed Martinis with the same enthusiasm for ritual he gave to carving the Thanksgiving turkey, but he occasionally introduced unconventional ingredients such as anisette or fruit juice and was said to be a sloppy mixer. (His secretary, Grace Tully, said that FDR once absentmindedly made a Martini of aquavit instead of gin.) Dean Acheson, then Acting Secretary of the Treasury, recalled drinking Martinis with FDR: The lid on the cocktail shaker spout was missing, so the president held his thumb over the spout while shaking. (The president's favorite silver cocktail shaker engraved with palm trees is on display at the FDR museum at Hyde Park.) Harry Truman didn't drink Martinis, but his Secretary of State, Dean Acheson, did. David Acheson said his father

Statesman Dean Acheson liked to shake the hell out of his gin Martinis.

OBSERVER: "THE MARTINI SCANDAL"
BY RUSSELL BAKER

This all happened at lunch the other day at the table of The Six Borgias and a man who was there swears it's the truth.

Four of those scrupulously barbered executive types who buy and sell actors and fly around on jets had settled into a table that counted and Ivo, the suave Yugoslav waiter from Akron, came to take their drink orders.

"I'll have a Tanqueray martini with a slice of lemon peel," says one. "Make mine a Lamplighter on the rocks," says another. "Vodka martini, extra dry," says the third, "and make sure the vodka is Polish."

"And yours, sir?" Ivo asked the fourth man.

"I'll have a martini," he says.

"I beg your pardon," says Ivo.

"A martini."

"What kind of martini?" asks Ivo.

"I don't care," the fellow says. "Just a martini."

One of his companions, sensing the start of a social crisis, moved helpfully to head it off. "Bill," he says, "maybe you'd like an American vodka martini, seven-to-one, with California vermouth and an olive stuffed with anchovy."

"No," says Bill. "Really, all I want is just a martini." And, apparently feeling that the subject was closed, he turned to the fellow on his right and started talking about tax-free municipals.

Ivo's face by this time was a study in despair, but being a discreet waiter, he glided off to the bar. In a few minutes he returned with the bartender. "About your martini, sir," the bartender says to Bill. "How do you feel about a Beefeater extra dry with a twist of lemon and rocks on the side?"

"Oh, I don't care," says Bill, "as long as it's a martini." And he resumed his conversation, which by this time dealt with some skyscrapers he was buying as a tax dodge. The bartender, who had been hired at great expense because he was famed for his temperament, flew off in a rage to give the *maitre d'hôtel* his resignation.

Soon, the *maitre d'hôtel* returned to the table with Ivo and the bartender in train and turning his most oleaginous smile on Bill, purred, "In regard to the Signor's martini . . . ."

"Yes," says Bill, "I'd like to have it right now."

"If I may take the liberty to suggest, Signor, our bartender, Cesare here, makes the most exciting bourbon Americano in North America, which I am certain Signor will find far more gratifying than a martini."

"I don't want bourbon," says Bill. "I want my martini."

"With an olive?" asks the *maitre d'hôtel*.

"It doesn't make any difference."

"Eight to one?"

"However you make them."

"Have a Limehouse yellow gin," says one of Bill's companions. "With South American vermouth," says another. "It's what everybody's drinking on Madison Avenue this week."

"And have it served in a frosted Madeira glass," the third man suggests, "with a sprig of parsley."

"Or with tiny pearl onions," the *maitre d'hôtel* suggests, kissing his fingertips. "The table of The Six Borgias uses only the choicest onions from Andalusia. They have been marinated for four years in Icelandic herring brine to bring out the juniper essence of Limehouse's quality gin."

"It's nice of you all to plan my martini for me," Bill says, "but I think I'll just have it regular."

Ivo glared. Cesare glared. The *maitre d'hôtel* glared. The three retreated for a conference behind a Michelangelo sculpture. They telephoned the owner. "Just give him any old gin you've got around the place and a little vermouth in a cocktail glass," the owner said.

"But suppose it leaks to the press," said the *maitre d'hôtel*. "We'd be the laughing stock of the overpriced restaurant racket."

"I'll be right over," said the owner. He arrived shortly afterward with a large sergeant of police. "What seems to be the trouble here?" the sergeant

Drawing by Stan Hunt;
© *1975 The New*
Yorker Magazine, Inc.

"And make that Martini executive size."

asks Bill. "This man insists on making a scene," says the *maitre d'hôtel.*

"All I want, sergeant, is a martini," says Bill.

"Oh," says the sergeant, "one of those troublemakers. Now, are you going to leave quietly or do we run you in for creating a disturbance in a public accommodation?"

"Throw him out!" cried Bill's companions, who were now confronted with the shattering probability of never again being able to get a table that counted. "The bum probably doesn't have a credit card," said the owner as Bill was shown the door.

"Now, sergeant," he said, "what about a little refresher?"

"Don't mind if I do," said the sergeant. "Make it a ten-to-one on the rocks, with Italian vermouth and three lime seeds in a chilled water tumbler lined with cheesecloth. And see that he stirs it exactly seven times."

(*New York Times*, May 16, 1965)

"liked drinking something transparent after all the murky transactions of statecraft." He never wanted them stirred, always shaken vigorously with plenty of ice. When someone worried if it would bruise the gin, Acheson replied, "I want to bruise the *hell* out of the gin!"

John Kennedy drank lightly, usually daiquiris, but he liked to see his friends drinking Martinis. Paul B. Fay, Kennedy's Under-Secretary of the Navy, remembers: "One day when both our wives were away, Jack invited me up to the White House. 'Say, Redhead—that's what he called me—why don't you have a Martini?' I asked if he wanted one, too, and he said, 'No thanks. I just like the idea of you drinking a Martini because I know it makes you happy.' And he was right. That was part of his charm, knowing what made people feel good. By the way, I still drink Martinis."

Though the Martini was the traditional power drink in the sixties, it was not immune to technological subterfuge. After all, this was the era of J. Edgar Hoover's wiretaps, Soviet surveillance, and James Bond's gadgets. San Francisco private eye Hal Lipset was called before a 1965 Senate sub-committee to give testimony on eavesdropping. Lipset's personal position was that since the government increasingly invaded citizens' privacy, the individual had to be ready to fight fire with fire. In Patricia Holt's *The Bug in the Martini Olive* (1991), Lipset explained how he and a colleague developed a bugged Martini:

> *The glass held a facsimile of an olive, which could hold a tiny transmitter, the pimento inside the olive, in which we embedded the microphone, and a toothpick, which could house a copper wire as an antenna. No gin was used—that could cause a short.*
>
> *Our point was that a host could wander through his own party, having drunk his own martini, and pick up the conversations that were directed at him, or leave his glass near a conversation he could then monitor in secret. We wanted to show the vast proliferation of this equipment, and the bug in the martini olive was one very fashionable example of many.*

Private eye Hal Lipset (center) showed two U.S. senators a bugged Martini glass and other eavesdropping devices in 1965.

After Lipset gave a demonstration, the Senators were fascinated by the spying Martini, and asked whether it would work with real gin in the glass, with an onion, or with a lemon peel.

> *They were so entranced with the idea that I couldn't help romanticize it a little. A Gibson, a lemon peel, sure; gin would not work but maybe vodka. . . . Things got very congenial all at once, and then when the reporters and photographers rushed up to get a photo, we were all laughing at how funny it was. I felt I had introduced a new toy, like a play-chew for a dog. They couldn't stop gnawing at it.*

For months afterward the media wrote about "the Tattler Martini" and "the Spy Martini." A cartoon in a magazine depicted two executives star-

Jock McDonald, American Martini, 1994, polaroid transfer print, 10 x 18 inches. (Modernism Gallery, San Francisco)

Bert Stern, Smirnoff Martini and Pyramid, *1955, color print from transparency, 30 x 30 inches. Stern shot this in Giza, Egypt.*

ing in horror at the Martinis set before them in a men's club. "Before we talk," one whispers to the other, "check for antennas." *San Francisco Chronicle* columnist Art Hoppe wrote, "To think that the martini, to which harried man turns for solace and comfort, should now turn on him . . ."

Bebe Rebozo used to make a classic "In and Out" Martini for Richard Nixon, who liked his Martinis about seven to one. Rebozo would

Richard Nixon

pour vermouth into the shaker of ice, swing it around once, and ceremoniously empty it before adding the gin. Nixon would laugh heartily, take the first long swallow, and mutter, "That's very good, Bebe. *Very* good." He reportedly was drinking Martinis the night the Watergate crisis drove him from office. Gerald Ford was a steady Martini drinker until his doctor gave him a choice of giving up ice cream or Martinis.

Drawing by Levin;
© 1978 The New
Yorker Magazine, Inc.

"The three-Martini lunch looks good."

THE THREE MARTINI DEBATE
BY CHRISTOPHER BUCKLEY

"They both come to my house. We serve them a Martini. And we have an exchange between the two."—*Tom Brokaw in* The New York Times, *proposing an alternative presidential debate format.*

BROKAW: Mr. President, Governor, thank you for coming. I'm sorry Mr. Perot declined, but he's a teetotaller. How do you take your Martinis?

BUSH: Dry as a bone, with fruit, and on the rocks.

CLINTON: I'll just have a beer, thanks.

BUSH: Whoa, what is this, Miller Time? I thought we were going to be hefting Martoonis.

CLINTON: Where I grew up, in a place called Hope, people drank corn liquor. Gin was for country clubs.

BUSH: I wouldn't start in on country clubs if I'd got *my* putter caught

in a wringer for belonging to an all-white club. If you see what I'm *driving* at . . . heh-heh.

CLINTON: I was never in that club. O.K., maybe I played a little golf there with businessmen, so I could target a few incentives on them. We can't all buy infrastructural investments out of our trust funds, ya know.

BROKAW: How do you want your Martini, Governor?

CLINTON: In a beer glass. Olives on the side. Got any peanuts or crackers?

BUSH: What's the matter? Got the munchies?

CLINTON: Tom, I govern better stoned than he does straight. Not that I ever did get stoned.

BUSH: Hold on. But I'm glad the subject of peanuts came up, because I think everyone in our wonderful country remembers Mr. Peanut, from Plains.

BROKAW: Your point being, sir?

BUSH: Exactly. Mmm. I'll have another. Little less vermouth this time.

CLINTON: Thank you, Tom. First, Al Gore and I happen to believe that there is a place for mixed drinks in today's post-New Deal Democratic Party. So I'll have another, too. Second, I'm proud to have an environmentally aware running mate who's orthographically sensitive to basic tubers. Third, could I get some more olives? In Arkansas we're working closely with the horticultural community on issues of olive-grove deforestation.

BUSH: Thank you. Mmm. Much better. Still a little wet, but getting there. I'd like to ask the Governor what he drank over there while he was learning social engineering at Oxford during the Vietnam War. *Draft* beer? Oh, Bar, Poppy's throwing ringers tonight!

CLINTON: That's been gone into again and again, so I'm not going to go into it. Could I get another, with olives?

BUSH: You know, Tom, after I was shot down by the Japsters while serving my country, which Governor Elvis here wouldn't know about, I was paddling like a wet cocker spaniel in those shark-infested waters down there. Not fun. Know what I couldn't stop thinking about? Aside from that fellow some people don't like to talk about—G-O-D? Wrapping my lips around an ice-cold see-through. How about

Drawing by Richard Decker; © *1949, 1977 The New Yorker Magazine, Inc.*

another. *Thirsty* just thinking about getting shot down.

CLINTON: Tom, it's hard to enjoy getting tanked when so many people in this country can't afford gin. The Germans and the Japanese are way ahead of us in terms of gin availability per capita, and Japan has the highest gin-to-vermouth ratio in the world.

BUSH: Seems to me the last Diberal Lemocrat, capital "D," capital "L," we elected was also anti-Martini.

CLINTON: There you go again with that negative stuff. O.K., one more. And keep those olives coming, Dan—er, Tom.

BUSH: Just wave the vermouth bottle over the glass. Don't even have to take the cap off. That's how Uncle Herbie used to make 'em. So where were we? Losing track. Out of the looped.

CLINTON: Isaiah Berlin used to say that Hank Williams was like a fox but Elvis was a badger.

BUSH: Berlin, *great* city. Wall. Down. But didn't see any foxes there and darn sure didn't see any badgers. Ah. *Thank you. Mmm* . . . Now *that's* a Martini. Just the way Gorbachev liked his. How do you think I got him to give up the Commie thing? That's right, gave him Uncle Herbie's recipe. *Worked.*

CLINTON: The Germans are way ahead of us on all walls. For failed Quayle four years of . . . I don't know who's driving home, but it better not be me. That's why I'm proud to have Al Gore for my designated driver.

BUSH: Gotta say, Hillary—a fox. Hair band, love it. Tipper—more of a badger, maybe, but still, *good woman.*

CLINTON: Hey, weren't we supposed to have some TV cameras here?

BUSH: Hold on, *por favor.* That was all worked out ahead of time. So don't cry for me, Bosnia-Herzegovina. But, Tom, gotta say, good format. If you gotta debate, this is how to do it. (*The New Yorker*, 1992)

In his pre-presidential days, a young actor named Ronald Reagan consoled Bette Davis with three Martinis when she played a self-destructive heiress in **Dark Victory, 1939.**

Along with the killer rabbit incident (on a canoe trip Carter swatted a disoriented swimming rabbit with a paddle) and his trip to Mexico (when he undiplomatically announced that he had suffered from Montezuma's Revenge), President Jimmy Carter's greatest misstep was attacking the mythical indulgence known as the "Three-Martini Lunch." It began during the peanut-growing populist's 1976 campaign, when Carter denounced the fat-cat businessman's habit of deducting "$50 Martini lunches" on the expense account, while blue-collar workers could not deduct the sandwiches in their lunch boxes. In a 1977 issue of *Time*, Hugh Sidey wrote:

One of the more spirited questions around Washington now is whether Jimmy Carter has ever had a three-Martini lunch. Hamilton Jordan, his top aide, has never seen Carter drink even one Martini. But Jordan says rather wickedly that he does not know what goes on over in the private part of the mansion after work.

Mary Hoyt, Rosalyn Carter's assistant, is quite firm in her conviction that not a single Martini has been mixed in the White House since the Carters arrived. It was Rosalyn, after all, who said out loud that she really enjoyed seeing "people kind of squirm" because there was no liquor served in the White House.

Press Secretary Jody Powell has never witnessed a Martini pass the presidential lips. However, he thinks that Carter has tasted one. But there Carter's enthusiasm waned.

The Martini issue is very serious. A high priority in Carter's plan for tax reform is an assault on expense account dining that would allow only half the cost of a meal to be tax deductible. In his campaign Carter conjured up a vision of privilege and corruption by pointing out that a three-Martini business lunch was deductible but not the $1.50 bologna sandwich of a worker.

President Jimmy Carter, the Martini's greatest enemy, drinking iced tea in front of the White House, 1980.

Carter's attack raised a nationwide ruckus in the restaurant and hotel industry when it was shown that eliminating even this small part of a restaurant's luncheon receipts (usually around 5 percent) would mean firing waitresses, bartenders, and busboys in many urban eateries. The attack

was a country boy's jab at the sophisticated urban chin. "The Martini is a city dweller, a metropolitan," as Bernard DeVoto had written. "It is not drunk beside a mountain stream or anywhere else in the wilds."

"One has to conclude that Jimmy Carter's crusade is, really, against martinis, not against the revenue lost to the government by their deductibility in certain circumstances," commented William F. Buckley. "The martini, let's face it, has become a code word. References to the 'three martini lunch' are designed not so much to evoke anger at the prospect of a dollar per martini lost in revenue to the government. They are designed to point to a lifestyle against which all the complicated glands in Jimmy Carter's body boil in protest."

But by the time Ronald Reagan entered office in 1980, Washington—and the nation—seemed ready for glamor again, and the Martini spurned by the homespun Carters was back in style. Plenty of Reaganites drank Martinis and smoked cigars,

A vermouth ad by Peter Arno, 1957.

don't be a faddist; don't be a sadist.

A Dry Martini is *not* a hooker of gin or vodka. It's a cocktail. And what *makes* it a cocktail is a noticeable, taste-pleasing, *civilizing* proportion of Noilly Prat *Extra Dry* Vermouth.

don't stir without

NOILLY PRAT

BROWNE VINTNERS CO., INC., NEW YORK CITY, SOLE DISTRIBUTORS FOR THE U.S.A.

150   HOLIDAY

ODE TO A MARTINI DRINKER
by Sold Cober

Starkle, starkle, little twink,
Who the hell you are I think,
I'm not under what they call
The alcofluence of incohol.
I'm not drunk as thinkle peep,
I'm just a little slort of sheep.
Tee martoonis make a guy
Fool so feelish, don't know why
Rally don't know who's me yet
The drunker I stay the longer I get
So just one more to fill my cup,
I've all day sober to Sunday up.

but the Gipper himself had given up Martinis for weak gin and tonics that he rarely finished. His name was linked to the Martini in 1987, when a trade war nearly erupted over U.S. grain exports to Europe. *The New York Times* said, "Wits called this episode the 'martini war' when President Reagan recently retaliated against Europe's high grain tariffs with high tariffs on British gin and Greek olives, and about a dozen other epicurean delights." The battle was solved by diplomacy.

During the Bush administration, the era of Glasnost and Desert Storm, the chief's Martinis were mainly made with vodka; in a recent letter President Bush said he still likes a vodka Martini shaken and served straight up with a lemon twist.

Martinis are not popular in the Clinton White House. It has been rumored that Clinton at some point tasted a Martini, but no one has confirmed if he actually swallowed. In his satirical novel, *Thank You for Smoking*, Christopher Buckley describes a hated tobacco lobbyist eating a politically incorrect lunch at a 1994 Washington hotspot called Bert's: "You could drink hard liquor in the middle of a school day without people assuming you were an alcoholic underachiever. Strange how in America in the 1950s, at the height of its industrial and imperial power, men drank double-martinis for lunch. Now, in its decline, they drank fizzy water. Somewhere something had gone terribly wrong."

Two men are driving through suburbia one day when they see a pair of dogs copulating on a front lawn. One man says, "Gee, I wish I could get my wife to do it that way." The other says, "That's easy. Just give her three Martinis and she'll do it any way you want." The man says, "Well maybe I should try that." About a week later, they meet again and the man who had given the advice asks, "Well did you try the Martinis? How did you get along?" The man replies, "Well, I got along very well, but you were way off count—I had to give her five Martinis just to get her out on the front lawn."

Drawing by Peter Arno;
© 1956, 1974
The New Yorker
Magazine, Inc.

"This is a hell of a way to run a railroad! You call that a dry Martini?"

"It's Martini genocide at the White House," says Lloyd Grove of *The Washington Post*. "Most of the Clintonians drink white wine or get high on their own intellects. The only one that knows about Martinis is James Carville. He's so high-strung it takes two Martinis to make him normal."

Carville, Clinton's wily political consultant, is a dedicated Martini drinker. "Bombay Sapphire gin, about four parts to one part vermouth," he drawled over the phone to me. "The important thing is to get every-

thing really cold. I like vodka, but only straight with caviar. To me a vodka Martini is like saying a Bourbon margarita. It doesn't exist. It has to be gin."

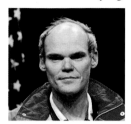

James Carville, the only Clintonian who likes Martinis.

Carville drinks gin Martinis at a political hang-out, the Palm Restaurant. "I'd say the only problem is they make 'em too big. Sometimes I worry about olives raising the temperature of the gin. And I like to taste the vermouth. None of this ten-to-one dry routine. To me the ultimate feeling in the world is to be about two-thirds of the way through my second Martini with people I like. Anything seems possible. Course by then my IQ has dropped to about 85. A cocktail has to look good, and to me there ain't a better looking drink than a Martini with an olive or a twist."

The Palm is, indeed, a classic place to drink Martinis. The walls are covered with caricatures of the regulars, from Teddy Kennedy to James Carville. On any given night (between indictments) you might see Dan Rostenkowski drinking his Martini garnished with two anchovy-stuffed olives. Kevin Rudowski, head bartender here for 16 years, says Martinis have made a strong comeback. "We're serving about half gin and half vodka martinis. Even the younger drinkers seem to be going back to gin. There are two secrets to a great Martini. The first is to use a well-chilled glass." What's the second? "I can't tell you. It's my own secret recipe."

A dry Martini with a twist of lemon was a staple at the Stork Club in Manhattan in the 1940s. (John William Lund photograph)

Congressman Dan Rostenkowski

During testimony before the Fulbright Committee in 1962 Senator William Fulbright asked, "Mr. Ambassador, how important is popularity to an American ambassador?"

Ambassador Ellis Griggs: "Mr. Chairman, popularity is all right if you like it, but it's like the olive in the martini: it just takes up space that could otherwise be used for gin."

"I made him a third Martini, but the women came and made us eat something, which spoiled a very promising evening." — ***Russell Baker,*** **The New York Times,** ***August 28, 1979***

Chapter Five

THE GREAT REVIVAL:

The Martini Is Dead... Long Live the Martini!

TO DEFINE WHAT THE MARTINI IS, PERHAPS IT'S WORTH determining what the Martini *isn't.* In his meditative *Mythologies* (1972), French philosopher Roland Barthes proposed that in France milk might be considered the opposite of wine. What, then, is the American opposite of the Martini?

Coca-Cola—naturally. While Coca-Cola is meant for the masses, the Martini is for the connoisseur who associates it with an elite group that roams from corporate boardrooms to country clubs. Coca-Cola is dark as coal, sweet as molasses, yet effervescent; the Martini is clear, innocent in its purity, but packs a powerful wallop. Coca-Cola is nonalcoholic, a liquid candy for a nation high on eternal youth, a daytime drink to be sipped through a straw at a baseball game. The Martini is a powerful intoxicant usually consumed in a softly lit bar long after the exertions of sport (but

Gus Heinze, **You've Earned It,** ***1994, acrylic on gesso panel, 26 x 26 inches. (Modernism Gallery, San Francisco)***

possibly before the passions of bed). Coca-Colas are for kids in puberty; Martinis are for adults contemplating power, sexual possibilities, or death. Coca-Cola gives the drinker a sugary giddiness; the Martini brings on dreams of once-and-future prosperity, heated romance, or maudlin murmurings, and eventually a longing for sleep.

Coca-Cola is premixed—thus unchanging, always promising the same experience for the individual, even over a lifetime; its formula has been kept secret by the monolithic company for a century. The soft drink comes ready-made; its red-and-white packaging is recognized throughout the world. And every Coca-Cola is made by a machine.

Every Martini is handmade, therefore personal, always unique. Unlike the Coca-Cola, the Martini's ingredients are well-known—vermouth and gin—but they gain mystery in their ritualistic blending. Where the Coca-Cola drinker must accept the limitations of the product, the Martini drinker can look forward to freedom through artistic bartending.

Bombay Sapphire Gin asked well-known designers to contribute unique glasses to their 1992 advertising campaign. This one is by Adam Tihany.

It's the right Vermouth that makes your Martini better

© RENFIELD IMPORTERS, LTD., N.Y.

MARTINI & ROSSI

M&R IMPORTED EXTRA DRY VERMOUTH

Martini & Rossi advertisement, 1952.

Despite its joys and blessings, the Martini appeared, not so long ago, to be on the verge of extinction. In 1978 a die-hard gin Martini drinker named Jefferson Morgan wrote a mournful article in *Bon Appetit* that began, "Now I come before you with a heavy heart to ring the tocsin of the end of civilization as we have known it. The true Martini cocktail stands in jeopardy of becoming one with the passenger pigeon, the dodo, and the St. Louis Browns, a situation clearly analogous to the decadence of Rome shortly before the fall of the Empire."

Yet just fifteen years later, the Martini—at least the vodka version—is on the upswing. Why? "A whole generation has become bored reciting, 'I'll

THE BOMBAY SAPPHIRE MARTINI. AS INTERPRETED BY ADAM TIHANY.

POUR SOMETHING PRICELESS.

Bombay® Sapphire™ Gin. 47% alc/vol (94 Proof). 100% grain neutral spirits. ©1992 Carillon Importers, Ltd., Teaneck, N.J. ©1992 Adam Tihany.

*Mark Adams, Martini,
1993, watercolor and
colored pencil on paper,
22 3/4 x 21 1/2 inches.
(John Berggruen
Gallery, San Francisco)*

just have a glass of white wine,' and then having something set in front of them that tastes foul and has no kick," says Ed Moose, proprietor of Moose's in San Francisco.

Some bartenders say that it represents a return to protocol and tradition, others see it as post-modern self-indulgence. For whatever reason, so many more Martinis are being shaken that some bartenders even complain of a mixologist's version of tennis elbow. My favorite place in New York City is the Oak Room at the Plaza Hotel, where the glasses are always chilled. The Temple Bar downtown is also good. As for Los Angeles, screen-

An Anonymous Inter-office Memo Circulated in 1967

The Martini menaces our civilization as much as the atom bomb.

It may be slower, but eventual destruction will be just as absolute. It wrecks more marriages than adultery, breaks up as many families as divorce, slays romance and causes unemployment. It remains undefeated, the eternal champion, the ferocious opponent of all mankind. Only the foolishly courageous try to drink this wicked cocktail, but there isn't a lush alive who doesn't believe he can win a decision over the slam of olive-tainted poison.

The Martini lushes, unlike the other species of rummy, seldom get surly or stormy. They fall through their clothes and become imbedded in a coma that suggests a guy who has been bored to death. Lined up against a bar, they resemble a rack of hand-me-down suits in a second-hand gents furnishing store. They are useless and cease to function as human beings after the fifth dose.

The Martini is the great equalizer. The greatest beauty turns into an open-mouthed, bleary-eyed blob of flesh. They, men and women alike, become remote with the vague numbness of idiocy. Conversation ceases as the vocal chords become paralyzed with the other organs of the body. The I.Q. of a Martini stiff is the lowest in the world. The Martini produces neither dreams, excitement, nor jollification.

It is my belief there is only one form of life lower than a horse player. That's a horse player who also drinks Martinis.

Lapel button c. 1950.

*Following pages: Classic
shakers including a red
glass lady's leg, two 1936
penguins, a rooster, a
1930 zeppelin, and a
magnificent 1930
airplane shaker that sold
at auction for $3,200.
Photo: John William Lund
(From the collections of
Robert Greenberg and
Richard Fishman)*

Bernard Schoenbaum

writer Mark Miller says most of the city suffers from Martini amnesia. "The only good bartenders are the oldtimers at Chasen's, Musso & Frank, and the Polo Lounge. When I want a great Martini, I fly to San Francisco for a cold one at Alfred's Steakhouse, Fog City Dinner, or at Bix."

San Francisco may be the most Martini-conscious city in the United States. "Professor" Jerry Thomas reputedly made the first Martini in the 1860s at the old Occidental Hotel (on Montgomery Street until the 1906 quake). Today the new Occidental Grill (established 1992) on Pine Street has become a hotspot for Martini-drinkers. One evening over Martinis their principal barman Steve Zell reverently displayed a vintage edition of Jerry Thomas' 1887 bar manual. "Jerry Thomas used to call his customers 'patients.' I like that! It is my belief that no civilized man or woman should be able to make it from the street to our dining room without first stopping for a Martini at the bar. It's the only sensible thing to do."

Zell offered a couple of pointers on making the Great One. "The coldest Martini is always the best Martini. We keep our glasses in the freezer. We put our vermouth in first, shake it into the ice, then pour it out before putting in the gin or vodka."

Drawing by Phil Frank, from Art Hoppe's column in the San Francisco Chronicle.

A few minutes later, a young filmmaker named Peter Moody came up to the bar to talk with Zell. Moody was shooting what he called a docufiction entitled *Olive or Twist.* "It's about a bike messenger who develops an obsession for the Perfect Martini. He talks to a lot of bartenders, starts wearing suits, even goes to the Martini & Rossi factory in Italy, and gets sophisticated. In the end he comes full circle." Moody was dressed in a cap emblazoned with a Martini glass and a black sweater with a giant Martini glass across the

Claes Oldenburg, Tilting Cocktail, 1983-84, stainless steel, cast aluminum, acrylic paint, and plexiglass, 19 inches tall, edition of 50. Photo: D. James Dee. (Brooke Alexander Editions, New York)

front. Zell tried to buy the sweater, but Moody said, "I can't sell it. My mom knitted it for me."

According to the Distilled Spirits Council, the vodka Martini, though spurned by traditionalists, is now the most popular mixed drink in Washington, D.C. And it is vodka that has brought the Martini back to popularity among young drinkers. Even as the Cold War escalated, the clear Russian liquid was infiltrating the bars and kitchens of America. Vodka imports jumped from 51,000 gallons in 1976 to 5 million today.

The Martini's resurgence is more than just marketing expertise aimed at a generation of yuppies weary of wine or cocaine. It represents a return to style and tradition. For those who grew up in the fifties with parents who cha-cha-ed to the icy music of a Martini shaker, drinking a Martini

"MARTINI-DRINKING HUSBAND"
BY ABIGAIL VAN BUREN

DEAR ABBY: My husband is a radiologist. He's a wonderful husband and an excellent provider, but he has some peculiar ideas.

For example, when we go out for an evening, he orders a vodka martini with eight olives. If for some reason he doesn't get the eight olives, he cancels the order and asks me to leave with him, which is very embarrassing.

This is not the worst of it. If he gets the olives, one by one he puts them in his nose and sniffs out the juice. He claims it clears his sinuses.

I don't mind when he does this at home, but when he does it in public, I want to crawl into a hole.

He doesn't have any allergies or sinus trouble, so I can't see the sense of this. Should he find a psychiatrist?
RADIOLOGIST'S WIFE

DEAR WIFE: Yes, but he should find one who drinks martinis with a twist of lemon so they won't fight over the olives.

Edward Ruscha, **Empty Glass,** *1994, acrylic on paper, 14 ½ x 11 ½ inches. Photo: Paul Ruscha. (Modernism Gallery, San Francisco)*

is nostalgic reincarnation. Los Angeles artist John Register told me, "When I was young and rebellious, I rejected the Martini and all it stood for. Now I like to drink them. My fondest memory of the Martini relates to my stepfather. When dinner was served, he would toss the undrunk portion of his Martini into the fireplace. There would be a pyrotechnic *woof* off the eucalyptus logs, and we children would marvel at the jet fuel that propelled our parents."

The Martini is to upper-middle class WASP society what peyote is to the Yaqui Indians: a sacred rite that affirms tribal identity while providing a nice high either at home or in a public place. As Lowell Edmunds observed:

Stephen Visakay of West Caldwell, New Jersey, owns 950 cocktail shakers, the largest collection in the world.

> *The adult, upper-class, optimistic male does not regard the past as something bad. He has ties to the past, one of which is the Martini. His earliest recollections of this drink may be connected with his father's college reunions or of a cocktail party that he happened to attend as a child, at which he saw the pillars of the community drinking the cold, clear drink in stemmed glasses. To such a man, the Martini that he drinks is a form of communion with his ancestors. The Martini is the living past.*

One might see the Martini as an extended metaphor for Euro-American culture itself. Gin's history is Dutch and English—and from these countries came the dominant ethnic groups that settled North America, signed the Declaration of Independence, and created the greatest capitalist society in the world. Invented in Napoleonic times, French vermouth calls to mind the Louisiana Purchase; indeed this beverage entered America through New Orleans. Italian vermouth's move from sweet to dry mirrors the Italian immigrant's assimilation. The lemon is the Caribbean or

Lowell Edmunds, author of **The Silver Bullet** *(1981), is a classics professor at Rutgers University. (Jack Abraham photograph)*

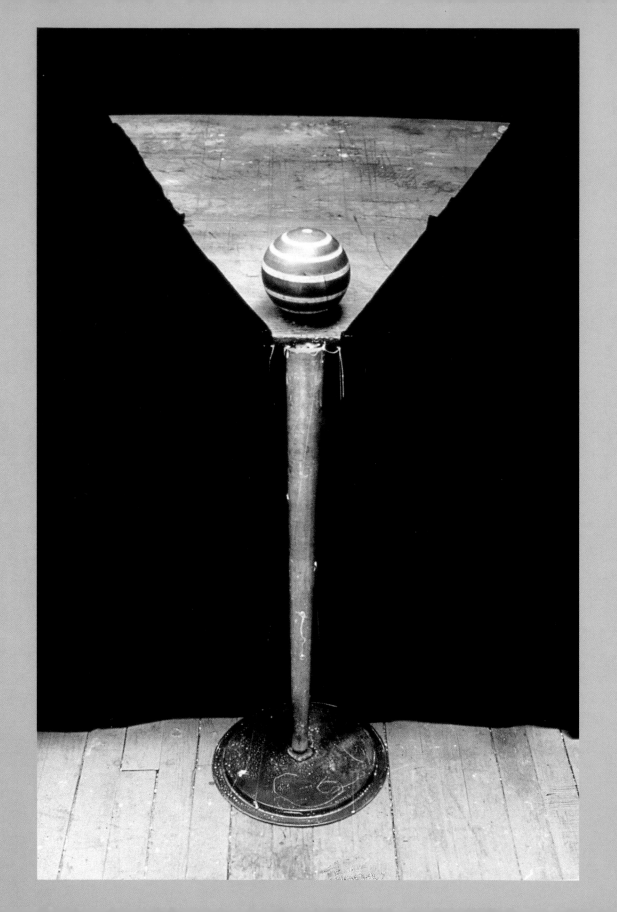

Zeke Berman, Martini, 1985, gelatin silver print, 32 x 28 inches. (Modernism Gallery, San Francisco)

Latin American culture, while the olive is Italian or Greek, and the pickled onion German or Jewish. The switch to vodka predates Perestroika and Glasnost but cannot be separated from America's Cold War fascination with Russian and Eastern European politics. As Bernard DeVoto wrote:

Our forebears were a tough people; nothing so clearly proves it as that they survived the fearful mixtures they drank. A defect of their qualities, I suspect, led them into abomination. They had the restless mind, the instinct to experiment and make combinations that produce inventions. We got radar from that instinct, and Congress, and the Hearst press, and many other marvelous or mysterious works. And we got, four generations ago, mixtures of all the known ferments and distillates in every combination that whim, malice, or mathematics could devise. When the instinct reached an apex of genius, we must remember, it flowered into the martini.

Neo-Martini Culture in San Francisco: Restaurateur Doug "Bix" Biederbeck, writer Barnaby Conrad III, art dealer Martin Muller, artist Mark Stock, restaurateur Bill Higgins, investor Ann Moller, and San Francisco Chronicle columnist Herb Caen drink Alan Cohen's Martinis at Bix Restaurant. (Jock McDonald photograph)

"You can no more keep a Martini in the refrigerator than you can keep a kiss there. The proper union of gin and vermouth is a great and sudden glory; it is one of the happiest marriages on earth, and one of the shortest-lived. The fragile tie of ecstasy is broken in a few minutes, and thereafter there can be no remarriage."

— *Bernard DeVoto,* Harper's, *1949*

CHAPTER SIX

MIXING THE PERFECT MARTINI

THE NOTION OF A PERFECT, INVIOLATE MARTINI HAS stirred (or shaken) the imagination for most of this century, and everyone, it seems, has an opinion about how a Martini should be made.

Consider this joke that developed after World War II. An American pilot bails out over the Sahara, and finds himself in the desert with nothing around for miles. Several days pass and he loses hope. Finally, he opens his survival kit and finds a box marked "Dry Martini." The box holds flasks of vermouth and gin, a shaker, and a freeze-dried twist of lemon. Just as he's shaking up a morale-boosting cocktail, a Bedouin gallops up on a camel and sneers, *"That's no way to make a Martini!"*

Opposite: Shaking it up at the Park Lane Bar, famed for the sensual Howard Chandler Christy murals.

In *The Silver Bullet*, Lowell Edmunds describes the delicate cultural balancing act the Martini represents, and how it reflects our fragile civilization:

When the Martini could be prepared by sloshing gin over ice cubes in a glass, with perhaps a dash of vermouth, ceremony was no longer required or even possible. The casualness of the Martini on the rocks obviously corresponds to many other changes in the social life of the 1960s, that decade of riots, assassinations, and war. In the history of the Martini, the Martini on the rocks represents the ultimate denial of the classic, civilized Martini and its rite, a denial already foreboded in the movement toward a "naked Martini," a Martini consisting of pure gin.

What shocked Edmunds fifteen years ago would now drive him deeper into depression. In the spirit of experimentation, drinkers have not only added ingredients such as grenadine, Sherry, absinthe, cider, coffee liqueur, or Chanel No. 5, but also such garnishes as—horrors!—tiny shrimp, green beans, anchovies, mint, watercress, pistachio nuts, artichoke hearts, red caviar, tiny eggplants, maraschino cherries, or crystallized violets. Other garnish perverts have dropped bacon bits or midget corncobs into the once-sacred elixir.

The Cajun Martini, as irreverent as the bite of a red ant, is made from peppered vodka served over a crushed jalapeño. There is also a Red Martini colored with Campari, and a Japanese variation combining vodka and sake. Bartenders report misguided members of an Anglophile cult ordering Gordon's gin with a splash of Pimm's Cup No. 1 and a slice of cucumber. On the opposite hand, there are ascetics who drink a plain "Charles Dickens" Martini—no olive or twist. (That faction would include my friend Bob Gardner, a San Francisco advertising guru, who states simply, "I don't do fruit.")

Serious tampering with the Martini has been going on for years. In 1951 a Chicago liquor dealer held a contest for variations on the Martini and received two hundred entries, including drinks made with sauterne, Scotch whiskey, and liebfraumilch. The winner was a Martini served in a glass rinsed with

If you don't have a watch, listen for shaking ice—five in the afternoon is cocktail hour.

New Orleans Chef Paul Prudhomme promoting his Cajun Martini in 1986.

Automation invaded Martini Culture in 1961 with the appearance of the push-button Cocktailmatic. As the original UPI photo-caption noted, "It is now possible for the host and hostess to drink all they like at their party, and still turn out perfectly proportioned cocktails. Their hands need only remain steady enough to push the right button." And it's smooth sailing to Blottoland.

Cointreau and garnished with an olive stuffed with anchovy. William Grimes records that in 1959 a Chicago restaurateur improbably named Morton C. Morton invented the Mortoni, which consisted of two bottles of gin and one ounce of vermouth garnished with a whole peeled Bermuda onion. Given that it was nearly two quarts of booze, Morton said it would be enjoyed "only by people with the most fashionable psychoses." That same year a bar in Washington, D.C., enjoyed fleeting notoriety for serving the "dillytini," a Martini garnished with a string bean pickled in dill vinegar.

Gilbey's Gin advertisement circa 1944.

For the most delicious Martini
in the world, make one with
the gin that for nearly a
century has been the
world's favorite

GILBEY'S

the International

GIN

John Nava, **Martini Study,** *1994, 12 x 10 inches. (Modernism Gallery, San Francisco) The picture is a pun on the postcard, which depicts a scene from the life of St. Martin, painted by the 14th century Sienese master, Simone Martini.*

Even a character in John Steinbeck's *Sweet Thursday* (1954) substituted Chartreuse for vermouth. David Embury, an eminent British mixologist, identified other Martinis including the Flying Dutchman made with a dash of curaçao, and an Allies Martini made with a dash of kümmel. With two dashes of absinthe and grenadine the classic drink becomes a Gloom Chaser Martini.

The self-congratulatory, oh-so-clever individual garnishes are doomed to be passing fancies. The classic dry Martini resists the intrusion of personality, and the fickle fads of a trend-tortured world.

Einstein would have had trouble defining a stable, chaos-free equation for the Perfect Martini. Mixing this drink is a highly personal act that is fraught with superstition and often verges on the pretentious. While some insist the vermouth must enter the pitcher before the ice and gin, others swear it must be shaken not stirred.

Why not stirred? "It bruises the gin," James Bond once explained.

Bond—that is, Ian Fleming—is directly contradicted by another Englishman, W. Somerset Maugham, who said, "Martinis should always be stirred, not shaken, so that the molecules lie sensuously on top of one another."

Whether stirred or shaken, a great Martini begins with good ingredients. Churchill insisted on drinking the gin especially made for his London club, Boodles. Most gins taste the same, with the exception of Bombay Sapphire. It is also still possible to get Boord's Old Tom Gin which has a sweeter taste. The personal favorite of Jeremiah Tower, owner of Stars Restaurant in San Francisco, is Booth's, a highly aromatic gin that, when served ice cold with Noilly Prat vermouth and a twist of lemon, is unbeatable. On the other hand, one of the best Martinis I've ever had is served by 80-ish Bruno Mooshei at the Persian Aub Zam Zam Room on Haight Street in San Francisco. Bruno uses Boord's gin, Boissière vermouth, and small (three-ounce) glasses that are highly chilled.

Also pick a good vermouth. Maugham was particular about this element, and wrote in 1958: "Noilly Prat is a necessary component of a

Maugham preferred his Martinis stirred, not shaken.

Since the first Dry Martini
as mixed Noilly Prat

dry martini. Without it you can make a side car, a gimlet, a white lady, or a gin and bitters, but you cannot make a dry martini." You can't go wrong with Noilly Prat. The big secret to vermouth is to use it fresh. Don't keep an open bottle for over a month.

Vodka was invented at least 800 years ago in either Russia or Poland, depending on which book you consult. It is drunk throughout Slav territory, in much of Scandinavia, in the Balkans, and as far east as Iran. There are factories in St. Petersburg that make flavors ranging from red pepper and lemon to chocolate and pepper. In spite of the Cold War with the Soviet Union, the late 1940s saw a growing market for vodka in the United States. For the most part vodka prepared for the American and European market is of great purity and without any flavor except that inherent to alcohol. This makes it dull to drink the Russian way—straight—but excellent for mixed drinks.

For the man or woman who likes the aromatic flavor and scent of gin but can't tolerate the effect of juniper berries on their emotions, I have a suggestion: fill a shaker with ice, pour in a jigger of gin, shake it briskly, pour off the gin, then fill it with vodka and vermouth. You'll transmit the scent of gin, but avoid its real or imagined effects on your brain.

The classic Martini consists of two ounces of gin mixed with one ounce of vermouth—a two-to-one ratio, *plus a dash of orange bitters* (a detail often forgotten today). You may certainly go drier—six-to-one is a good dry Martini—but any less gin than two-to-one means you're headed for what old-time purists call a Gin and French [vermouth].

Combine the blend with ice cubes in a classic silver shaker (or a glass shaker with silver top) and agitate vigorously until your hands nearly stick to the frost glazing the outside—about eight good shakes. Don't worry about bruising the gin. Strain the ice-cold results into

A young bar maid met the future—a cocktail robot—at a bartender's school in New York in 1933.

a Martini glass that has previously been chilled in the freezer. If you insist on stirring the gin, the ingredients may be mixed with ice cubes in a pitcher (also frosted in the freezer) and agitated with a long-handled spoon. Choose vigor rather than languor when the spoon is in hand.

A great Martini should be like skinny-dipping in a nordic lake with Greta Garbo. Teeth-chatteringly cold. To make a good Martini you need ice. Even if you keep your glass, your shaker, and your gin or vodka in the freezer (which I do), the ingredients must be shaken with ice cubes. The ice just takes the edge off the gin or vodka and weds it to the vermouth. (And do not use those silly plastic-coated ice cubes or metal ball-bearings.)

I was in Harry's Bar in New York recently and was disappointed on two counts: when I ordered a Martini, the bartender simply reached into the freezer and drew out a premixed Martini sitting in a small cylindrical whiskey glass. Sure it was cold, and sure the gin and vermouth were of the highest quality—but the drink had never even touched a cube of ice!

Drawing by Ross;
© 1984 The New
Yorker Magazine, Inc.

"Six Martinis. Mission accomplished."

At home you need a cold freezer to get ice cubes very hard, and you should use bottled spring water to avoid impurities in tap water. For a second round of Martinis toss out the old ice cubes and fill your shaker with fresh recruits. (Never store your vermouth in the refrigerator or in the freezer, where it will freeze; it is aromatic and does well at room temperature.)

The classic Martini glass is stemmed, about six inches high, not curved like a wine glass, but cone-shaped with straight sides. The interior well is curved at the bottom, conveniently accommodating an olive or onion pierced on a toothpick. Choose a glass that holds between three and four ounces, nothing bigger—it will allow you to have a second Martini without going over Inebriation Falls.

*Mel Ramos, **Martini Miss**, 1993, oil on linen, 64 x 48 inches. (Modernism Gallery, San Francisco)*

(Unfortunately, today's professional bar glasses tend to be much bigger, about six to eight ounces.) Ideally the glass will be as cold as ice, having spent twenty minutes in your freezer.

The Martini glass has become a talisman of thirties modernism with its art deco design, its reductionist boldness, and *Thin Man* elegance. It is as poised as a ballerina on point and its contents must be imbibed with care. When the barman sets the drink down, you take a moment to savor the minimalist presence as one might a Mondrian painting or a Brancusi sculpture. The Martini glass itself helps the drinker relax and change gears. Unlike whiskey served in a tumbler, the Martini cannot be belted back in

David Levinthal, **Untitled,** *1994, polaroid print, 24 x 20 inches. (Modernism Gallery, San Francisco)*

Barnaby Conrad III, **Mondrian's Martini,** *1992, oil on canvas, 10 x 8 inches.* **(Modernism Gallery,** *San Francisco)*

one toss — or at least not without losing much of it on your shirtfront.

High tradition calls for a twist of lemon. This does not mean a slice of lemon with pulp. It should just be a sliver of peel about 1 $^1/_2$ inches long trimmed to a quarter inch in width. Deftly crank the twist over the Martini's surface, allowing a few drops of fragrant lemon oil to dapple the limpid surface. You may also wish to use a spare peel to run around the lip of the glass for extra flavor. Then drop the twist into the cool depths. (Of course, some people insist that the twist must be at the bottom of the glass *before* the concoction is poured.)

The Martini drinker is often proud of arcane foibles and superstitions. He may be possessed of an ornery fastidiousness that only another Martini drinker would understand. "There are two classes of nonprofessional Martini-makers," M.F.K. Fisher said, "those who are rudely convinced nobody in the world can make one quite so well as they, and those who shy away from the bar and say with melodramatic modesty that they can ruin *anything*. The second, when pressed, usually make the better drink."

Consider this joke from the fifties about Martini fanaticism:

A man walks into a bar and says he wants a very, very dry Martini at a ratio of 25 to 1. The bartender is a little startled but mixes it precisely. As he pours it into just the right glass, he asks the customer, "Would you like a twist of lemon peel in that?" The customer pounds the bar and shouts, "Listen, buddy! When I want a goddamned lemonade, I'll ask for it!"

Bernard DeVoto was harsh on people who made Martinis with sweet vermouth or—worse—with garnishes other than lemon peel:

And, I suppose, nothing can be done with people who put olives in martinis, presumably because in some desolate childhood hour someone refused them a dill pickle and so they go through life lusting for the taste of brine. Something can be done with people who put pickled olives in: strangulation seems best.

"The man who first put the olive in the Martini should be shot," wrote a vengeful lemon twist stalwart in a 1934 *Esquire.* Don't listen to

David Salle, Gilbey's, 1993, oil and acrylic on canvas, 82 x 92 inches. (Gagosian Gallery, New York)

tyrannical blowhards. These days, heretics straying from the true lemon twist faith may, indeed, choose a green olive as garnish without risking derision or a life in mixological purgatory. In fact the olive has nearly re-placed the lemon peel as standard. As TV host Johnny Carson said in the 1960s, "Happiness is finding two olives in your Martini when you're hungry."

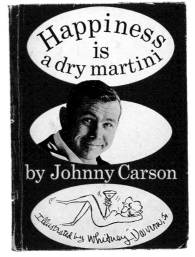

TV host Carson published this book in 1965.

Most bars use green olives stuffed with a pimento, but if you can, select smaller olives that have been pitted but not stuffed with anything. "The best are called *drunken olives*," says Doug Biederbeck of Bix Restaurant in San Francisco, "which means they come al-ready packed in vermouth." Then you must choose between skewering one or two on a toothpick, or letting a lone olive reign elegantly from the bottom of the glass. You want to eat the olive right away? Most people wait, but go ahead; it's even okay to ask the bartender for three olives at the outset.

When garnished with a pickled pearl onion, the Martini is known as a Gibson, endearingly called "onion soup." There are three stories about the origins of the Gibson. One has an American ambassador named Gibson serving in London during Prohibition. He wished to make his English guests welcome with a good cocktail, but personally felt constrained to follow his country's laws even while abroad. So during receptions he would circulate carrying a glass of water with a cocktail onion in it, while the guests would be served real gin. When someone asked his aide what the diplomat was drinking, the young man answered "a Gibson."

James Guçwa, The Martini Lounge, 1994, oil on canvas, 22 x 16 inches. (Modernism Gallery, San Francisco)

Steve Zell at the Occidental Grill in San Francisco says the name came out of Chicago. "You'll notice that Gibsons are usually served with two skewered onions. I heard that during the twenties in Chicago there were twin sisters named Gibson who loved Martinis but hated olives. Whenever they'd go out, they'd get the bartenders to use two pickled onions—twins for twins."

A more likely story is that Charles Dana Gibson, the famed illustrator

Drawing by W. Miller;
© 1977 The New
Yorker Magazine, Inc.

THE BIRTH OF THE MARTINI

and creator of the Gibson Girl, dropped into The Players, his New York club, and asked the bartender, Charley Connolly, to mix him "a better Martini." Connolly simply exchanged an onion for an olive and dubbed it the Gibson.

A black olive served in vodka is today known as a Buckeye Martini, but in the 1950s was nicknamed an "Althea Gibson" after the celebrated black tennis player.

Be careful with your toothpicks. The absentminded drinker may be in for trouble. The October 16, 1985 edition of the *New England Journal of Medicine* reported the strange case of one Daniel Malamud, a Philadelphia biochemist, who came home from work and mixed his customary Gibson Martini. While eating the onion, he accidentally swallowed the wooden toothpick. Panicking, he ran into the bathroom and made himself vomit. This vaulted the toothpick into his nasal passage. Waiting in the emergency room of Philadelphia's Lankenau Hospital, the poor man watched as the nurse wrote on the blackboard: *Malamud. Toothpick up nose.* "It was there among all those people who had been shot, battered, or beaten," said the patient with embarrassment. The toothpick was removed easily enough and a brief mention was made in the medical journal. (Malamud was luckier than Sherwood Anderson, author of *Winesburg, Ohio,* who succumbed to peritonitis after swallowing the toothpick from a Martini olive.)

The big choice, of course, is not so much between olives and onions or stirring and shaking but between gin and vodka. Aside from the James Bond books, the earliest written record of a vodka Martini appeared in a 1951 cocktail book, Ted Saucier's *Bottoms Up.* The recipe for a "Vodkatini" was contributed by Jerome Zerbe, photographer and then society editor of *Town and Country.* Zerbe called for $4/5$ jigger of Smirnoff vodka and $1/5$ jigger of dry vermouth to be stirred with ice; the garnish was a twist of lemon peel. Forty years ago, ordering a vodka Martini in an old-time bar was as radical as exploding a Molotov cocktail. Today it is purely a matter of taste.

Even if you don't mix your own drinks, an essential part of enjoying a Martini is its preparation. With professionalism and a dash of character, a masterful bartender elevates duty to craft, then to an art. Just as the priest at the altar washes his hands and transfers the sacred wine to the silver chalice, so a very good bartender confers something inexplicable, ineffable, and possibly divine, to the drink. Then it is up to the drinker to decide whether the Martini, when consumed in sufficient quantity, conjures a benevolent God or gods—or a destructive demon.

Tani Gazin, **Fourth of July,** *1994, watercolor on paper, 19 x 18 inches. (Modernism Gallery, San Francisco)*

Some insist the juniper essence in gin provokes mystical olfactory pleasures—and unexpected angers. My father, who once owned a San Francisco nightclub called El Matador, said that every time there was a fight in the club the protagonists invariably had been drinking Martinis. New York restaurateur Toots Shor called the Martini an "A-Bomb" and described its down side: "A guy comes in here and he looks like he's fresh from taking his lessons as an altar boy. He has one Martini and he wants to clean out the joint. A loving couple comes in; you never saw such a happy couple. Then the guy or the dame drinks a Martini and you've got to get the waiter to separate them."

The Martini is high-octane pleasure, but one is always flirting with danger. In his 1960 treatise *Social Drinking: How to Enjoy Drinking without Being Hurt By It,* Giorgio Lolli writes, "Its cool taste is almost indefinable, yet a martini's swift effects are multiplied by fatigue, low blood sugar, tensions, and anxieties. The Latin name, a perhaps unconsciously motivated misnomer, connotes the sudden potentialities of a drink which may favor rapid shifts from the stillness of self-control to the impetuosity of passion."

Martini Culture is not about getting stinking drunk and slipping under the table with a burp and a curse. It's about grace under pleasure. The idea is to make the rest of the evening more pleasant—not to obliterate it. Richard "Mr. Rick" Fishman, founder of San Francisco's floating party known

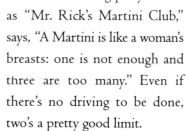

as "Mr. Rick's Martini Club," says, "A Martini is like a woman's breasts: one is not enough and three are too many." Even if there's no driving to be done, two's a pretty good limit.

Despite all the ritual, drinking a Martini is not about obeying rules or doing things the right way—it's about loosening up. As William Grimes wrote in *Straight Up or On the Rocks*, "The fretful neurotic who shakes up an after-work martini should emerge from the experience a changed human being: more generous and sociable, inclined toward deeper thought and the pleasures of the imagination."

Even if you go too far in drink there may be hidden benefits as J.A. Maxtone Graham demonstrates:

A party of thirty-six ladies from Stockton, California, were at the peak of their Martini happiness when two armed burglars broke in and announced at gunpoint that they would take away all the ladies' jewelry and money. There was no correct response from the party-makers, who merely asked the intruders to join them for a drink. Baffled by the whole affair, the burglars left empty-handed, and the party continued unabated.

So in all good faith, mix the best Martini you can, whether shaken or stirred, with gin or with vodka, with an olive or without, and just remember to put the cap back on the vermouth. Don't drink too fast. You've got all night, maybe all your life, before things get so bad a Martini can't help.

THE CLASSIC MARTINI

Pour 2 ounces of London dry gin, I ounce of French vermouth, and I dash of Fee Brothers' orange bitters into an ice-filled shaker. Shake, then pour into a well-chilled stemmed glass and garnish with lemon peel or olive. This is the way the Martini was made before Prohibition. (If you want a turn-of-the-century version, substitute sweet Italian vermouth for the French dry, and use equal proportions of vermouth and gin.)

THE MODERN DRY MARTINI

Pour 4 ounces of gin and $1/2$ ounce of dry vermouth into an ice-filled shaker. Shake, then strain into a glass. Garnish with a lemon twist or olive. An onion makes the drink a Gibson. Vodka may be substituted for gin to make a Vodkatini, but don't expect old-timers to appreciate it.

Rick Fishman, founder of Mr. Rick's Martini Club. (John William Lund photograph)

JAMES BOND'S MARTINI

Bond named the drink "The Vesper" for a beautiful double agent he loved. The recipe is 3 ounces of gin, I ounce of vodka, $1/2$ ounce blond Lillet, and a large, thin slice of lemon peel. Pour the liquid ingredients into an ice-filled shaker, shake, and strain into a Martini glass. Add the lemon peel, and keep your eyes peeled for enemy agents.

THE CAJUN MARTINI

Pour a fifth of your favorite gin or vodka into a large jug, jar, or bottle. Add two or three fresh jalapeño peppers (sliced, seeded, and deveined), and a single red chili pepper (don't overdo it!). Let sit in the refrigerator for two days. Shake with ice and vermouth in a 5 to I ratio. Serve straight up or on the rocks. (If too hot, dilute with more gin or vodka.)

Appendix I

A BRIEF HISTORY OF GIN

Franciscus Sylvius,
inventor of gin.

William III brought gin
to England in 1688.

Gin's origins go back to the Rennaissance. A late sixteenth-century Dutch professor of medicine, Franciscus Sylvius, has generally been credited with making the first gin, which he prescribed as a diuretic. Subsequent recipes traditionally included coriander seeds, orris, orange peel, cassia bark, lemon peel, cardamom capsules, angelica, caraway seeds, and juniper berries—called *genièvre* by the French—which is the foundation of gin's distinctive taste. Unlike bourbons and malt whiskeys, gin has an indirect chemical relationship with the grains from which it is derived; it is little more than diluted alcohol flavored with juniper and other plant extracts.

As *genièvre's* popularity grew among the Anglo-Saxons, they shortened its name to gin. Royal politics gave it acceptance in England. William of Orange, a Dutchman, became king of England in 1688 when his predecessor, James II, was exiled to France. Up until then, many of the wines and spirits of the day had come from France, but King William ended French trade and gave the English the right to distill spirits from native-grown grain. Gin consumption in England rose from an estimated half million gallons in 1690 to 5 million gallons in 1727. In the next decade it nearly quadrupled to 20 million gallons. Since England's population was then 6.5 million people, that's four gallons per person annually.

Most was consumed in London. Public drunkenness was epidemic in London, spurring Parliament to pass the 1736 Gin Act, an attempt to limit production and impose heavy taxes on legal trade. The law was no more successful than America's Prohibition Act two centuries later. Many distillers stopped making gin proper and put out a different but coarser spirit to escape the taxes. This was colloquially known as *Parliamentary Brandy* and sold under "brand" names calculated to evade the Gin Act: *Cuckold's Comfort, Last*

Dixie Belle Gin
advertisement from
1934.

GIN LANE.

Shift, Ladies Delight, and *Gripe Water* among many. By 1742 consumption had risen. Illicit gin shops flourished. Though some 12,000 people were arrested, the prisons were too crowded to hold more.

The 1736 Act was such a failure that it was repealed in 1742. When reasonable taxes were restored, it encouraged responsible distillers to produce sound gin and take pride in their craft. Booth's, founded in 1749, remains the oldest distiller of gin in England.

During that period, gin was usually drunk straight without ice, a rare commodity. Its crude production made for bitter results that were sweetened with sugar. Although Lord Byron declared that "gin and water is the source of all my inspiration," it took gin over a century to shed its reputation as a liquid opiate for slum dwellers. Young Charles Dickens wrote scornfully of "gin palaces," and his illustrator, George Cruikshank, a reformed alcoholic, also attacked them. Nevertheless, gin gradually found its way into the houses of the gentry. Eventually Royal Navy officers began mixing gin with their bitters and other cocktail ingredients. At one point Prime Minister Gladstone proposed to halve the number of public houses in England; the measure was soundly defeated in Parliament. Three years later when he lost at the polls, he commented that he had "been borne down in a torrent of gin."

It was not until the late-1800s that the English eliminated sugar in favor of a drier gin. Today, there are two basic kinds of gin, Dutch and London. The British variety is made in two steps. A fermented mash of grain (usually corn), rye, and malt are distilled, producing a nearly flavorless alcohol. The distiller then adds flavoring agents—the aromatic extracts of plants and herbs—and dilutes the mixture with distilled water to achieve the desired bottle proof. The Dutch practice a simpler process, putting in all the ingredients at the beginning so that the fermenting grain and flavoring agents intermingle and are distilled at a lower alcoholic level. For this reason, Dutch gin is considered more full-bodied and aromatic than London dry.

William Hogarth,
Gin Lane, *1750-51, engraving. This classic print shows the squalor that gin consumption caused in London during the eighteenth century. (New York Public Library)*

⟁

Appendix II

A BRIEF HISTORY OF VERMOUTH

Vermouth has some fifty ingredients and takes about four years to concoct and distill. It is made from wine fortified with alcohol and flavored with herbs and roots, including blessed thistle, forget-me-not, wormwood, and starwort. It is aged, decanted, filtered, refrigerated, clarified, and pasteurized to remove any floating material; the process renders the vermouth colorless.

Vermouth is an ancient liquor. The main ingredient is wormwood (*Artemisia absinthium*), a shrublike perennial with an aromatic odor that grows throughout Europe and Asia. Hippocrates recommended wormwood-steeped wine for jaundice and rheumatism in 500 B.C., and by the Renaissance it was sold in English apothecary shops as a medicinal.

The Piedmont region of Italy was a prime producer of modern vermouth. As early as 1678, Leonardo Fiorvanti wrote, "Vermouth is an aid to the digestion; it purifies the blood, induces sound slumber, and rejoices the heart." The oldest established vermouth house dates from 1757, but the earliest brand name appears in 1786, Carpano's *Punt e Mes*. This probably would have been a bittersweet vermouth—possibly as dry as we drink it today—but in the nineteenth century it became sweeter.

Today, the best known vermouth around the world is Martini & Rossi of Turin, Italy. The Martini & Rossi company began some time prior to 1840, and was originally known as Martini & Sola. The name change occurred when Commandatore Luigi Rossi gained co-ownership; under his

The author's father in a Lejon vermouth ad of the 1950s.

Gottfried Helnwein,
Martini, *1994, colored*
pencil on paper, diptych,
each image 18 ³/₄ x 16
³/₄ inches. (Modernism
Gallery, San Francisco)

four sons the company grew rapidly, particularly through innovative advertising. Although the company built its reputation on sweet Italian vermouth, it now dominates the market for dry French vermouth as well.

Historically, vermouth was the traditional *rosso* (red) variety, but around 1800 the Marseilles region of France began producing a dry white vermouth based on the white wines of the Midi. In 1812, the firm of Noilly Prat introduced a dry vermouth to France. The first bottle of Noilly Prat was shipped to America in 1851, arriving in New Orleans. By 1857, the liquor dealers of C.J. Edward and Company were hawking it in New York through druggists and apothecaries. After a slow start, by 1910 Noilly Prat was selling 75,000 cases a year in the United States. Today, it is considered the best vermouth available.

The major difference between Italian and French vermouths is the degree of sweetness. Italian vermouths have a reddish tone, not from any ingredient but from artificial color, while the French variety is a somewhat yellow color.

Mark Stock, Solo
Martini, *1994, oil on*
canvas on panel, 24 x
20 inches. (Modernism
Gallery, San Francisco)

BIBLIOGRAPHY

Baker, Russell. "Observer: 'The Martini Scandal,'" *The New York Times*, 16 May 1965.

———. "Observer," *The New York Times*, 28 August 1979.

Barthes, Roland. "Wine and Milk" from *Mythologies*. Translated by Annette Lavers. New York: Farrar Strauss, Giroux, 1972.

Bohlen, Charles E. *Witness to History: 1929-1969*. New York: W.W. Norton, 1973.

Bryan, J. III. "Martini Memoirs." *Signature*, November 1981, 64-74.

Buckley, Christopher. "The Three Martini Debate." *The New Yorker*, 12 October 1992, 120.

Buckley, William, F., Jr., "Reflections on the Martini Lunch." Syndicated column. 12 December 1977.

Buñuel, Luis. *My Last Sigh*. Translated by Abigail Israel. New York: Alfred A. Knopf, 1983.

Byron, O. H. *The Modern Bartender's Guide*. New York, 1884.

Carter, Jimmy. "Quotation of the Day." *The New York Times*, 18 February 1978.

Cheever, John. "The Five-Forty-Eight." In *The Collected Stories of John Cheever*. New York: Alfred A. Knopf, 1979.

Considine, Bob. "Expert Mixes Up a Philosophy on Martinis." *World Journal Tribune*, 5 April 1967.

DeVoto, Bernard. "For the Wayward and Beguiled." *Harper's* 199, no. 1195 (1949): 68-71.

Doxat, John. *Shaken—Not Stirred: The Dry Martini*. London: Hutchinson, Benham, Ltd., 1976.

———. *World of Drinks and Drinking*. London: Hutchinson, Benham, Ltd., 1976.

Edmunds, Lowell. *The Silver Bullet: The Martini in American Civilization*. Westport, Connecticut: Greenwood Press, 1981.

Embury, David A. *The Fine Art of Mixing Drinks*. Garden City, New York: Dolphin Books, 1961.

Fisher, M.F.K. "To the Gibson and Beyond." *Atlantic Monthly* (January 1949): 93-94.

Fitzgerald, F. Scott. "The Rich Boy." In *All the Sad Young Men*. New York: Scribner's, 1926.

Fleming, Ian. *Casino Royale*. New York: Macmillan, 1954.

Goodman, Ezra. *The Fifty-Year Decline and Fall of Hollywood*. New York: Simon & Schuster, 1961.

Graham, Maxtone J.A. "The Martini." *Gourmet* (November 1968): 27-46.

Grimes, William. *Straight up or on the Rocks*. New York: Simon & Schuster, 1993.

Hammett, Dashiell. *The Thin Man*. New York: Alfred A. Knopf, 1934.

Hemingway, Ernest. *Across the River and into the Trees*. New York: Scribner's, 1950.

———. *A Farewell to Arms*. New York: Scribner's, 1929.

———. *Selected Letters, 1917-1961*. Edited by Carlos Baker. New York: Scribner's, 1981.

———. *The Sun Also Rises*. New York: Scribner's, 1926.

Henry, O. *The Gentle Grafter*. 1904 Reprint, New York: Doubleday, Doran and Co., 1908.

Herzbrun, Robert. *The Perfect Martini Book*. New York: Harcourt Brace Jovanovich, 1979.

Holt, Patricia. *The Bug in the Martini Olive, and Other True Cases from the Files of Hal Lipset, Private Eye*. Boston: Little, Brown and Company, 1991.

Hoppe, Art. "Speak Directly into the Olive, Please," *San Francisco Chronicle*, 22 February 1965.

Johnson, Harry. *New and Improved Illustrated Bartender's Manual or How to Mix Drinks of the Present Style*. New York, 1888.

Keyes, Ralph. *Nice Guys Finish Seventh*. New York: HarperCollins Publishers, Inc., 1992.

Leonard, John. *The Naked Martini*. New York: Delacorte Press, 1964.

Lolli, Giorgio. *Social Drinking: How to Enjoy Drinking without Being Hurt by It*. Cleveland and New York: The World Publishing Co., 1960.

London, Jack. *Burning Daylight*. New York: Macmillan, 1910.

Maugham, W. Somerset. "The Fall of Edward Bannard." In *The Complete Short Stories*. London: William Heinemann, Ltd., 1951.

"Martini Heresy." *Life*, 10 December 1951, 81-82.

Morgan, Jefferson. "What Ever Happened to the Martini?" *Bon Appétit*, October 1978, 73-74.

Nash, Ogden. *Verses from 1929 On*. New York: Little, Brown and Company, 1935.

Palmer, C.B. "The Consummately Dry Martini." *The New York Times Sunday Magazine*, 6 April 1952, 41.

Saucier, Ted. *Bottoms Up*. New York: Greystone Press, 1951.

Sidey, Hugh, "In Defense of the Martini." *Time*, 24 October 1977, 38.

Smith, Jack. *Los Angeles Times*, 23 November 1992.

Stuart, Thomas. *Stuart's Fancy Drinks and How to Mix Them*. 1896. Reprint, New York: Excelsior Publishing House, 1904.

Tamony, Peter. "Martini Cocktail." *Western Folklore* 26, no. 1 (1967): 124-127.

Thomas, Jerry. *The Bar-tender's Guide*. New York: Dick & Fitzgerald, 1862.

———. *The Bon Vivant's Companion, or How to Mix Drinks*. Edited by Herbert Asbury. New York: Knopf, 1928.

Thomas, John. *Dry Martini: A Gentleman Turns to Love*. Reprint, Carbondale, Illinois: Southern Illinois University Press, 1974.

Tully, Grace. *F.D.R., My Boss*. New York: Charles Scribner's Sons, 1949.

Villas, James. "The Social Status of the Martini." *Esquire*, April 1973, 111-112.

INDEX

INDEX CONT'D